# Jesus

## Hero of
## Thy Soul

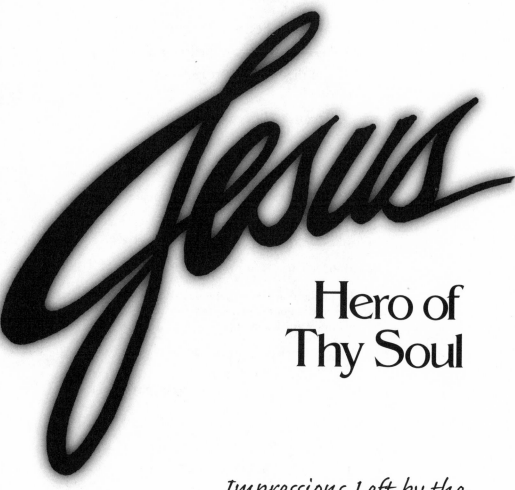

# Jesus

## Hero of
## Thy Soul

*Impressions Left by the
Savior's Touch*

# JIM MCGUIGGAN

HOWARD
PUBLISHING CO.

Our purpose at Howard Publishing is to:

- *Increase faith* in the hearts of growing Christians
- *Inspire holiness* in the lives of believers
- *Instill hope* in the hearts of struggling people everywhere

## Because He's coming again!

Published by Howard Publishing Co., Inc.,
3117 North 7th Street, West Monroe, Louisiana 71291-2227

98 99 00 01 02 03 04 05 06 07   10 9 8 7 6 5 4 3 2 1

**Library of Congress Cataloging-in Publication Data**

McGuiggan, Jim, 1937–
    Jesus, hero of thy soul : impressions left by the Savior's touch /
Jim McGuiggan
        p.  cm. —
        ISBN 1-878990-87-X
        1. Meditations.  I. Title.
        BV4832.2.M196   1998
        242—dc21                                                        98-9380
                                                                              CIP

Interior design by LinDee Loveland
Manuscript editing by Traci Mullins

✦

To my sister

Margaret (McGuiggan) Jaconette

whose light has shone all these years—
constant, bright, soft

# Contents

◆

Contents

♦

viii

Hero

ore than a

INTRODUCTION

# MORE THAN A HERO

Turn your eyes upon Jesus.
Look full in his wonderful face.
And the things of earth will
  grow strangely dim,
In the light of his glory and
  grace.

      —Helen H. Lemmel

     ◆

# More Than a Hero

✦

Let us fix our eyes on Jesus, the author
and perfecter of our faith.
Hebrews 12:2

N oted theologian P. T. Forsyth reminds us that Jesus is much more than a hero.[1] A hero relates only to our sense of admiration, but Christ also confronts the darkness in us—and deals with it.

When our eyes open to the Christ, even our admiration for him convicts us. His purity dazzles us without blinding; his strength awes us without driving us to grovel; his joy frees us without making us giddy or superficial. In our tender moments, we want to hug him for

3

what he did with the woman taken in adultery. And when we feel the need to be brave and speak out against injustice, our souls rise to their feet as he cleanses the temple or scathes the ruler of the synagogue who begrudged a satanic victim her freedom after eighteen years of bondage.

His "let there be light" to the man born blind opens our own eyes. When in Mark 2:12 people say, "We have never seen like this,"[2] we share their astonishment. It's more than "We have never seen anything like this"; it's "We have never *seen* like this." Life looks different because he gives us renewed vision.

He fulfills the words of Kipling as no other can:

> If you can talk with crowds and keep your virtue
> Or walk with kings and not lose the common
>      touch,
> If neither foes nor loving friends can hurt you,
> If all men count with you, but none too much . . .[3]

Only Jesus could give himself to all without pandering to anyone. Only he could treat us all as individuals while insisting that we belong to one another. Only he could forgive us fully, freely, gladly—but without dishonoring us or weakening our resolve for righteousness.

Having seen Jesus, knowing how he has lived his life here, we can't settle for less than a genuine pursuit of his likeness. His very presence among us forbids us to settle for just being "nice" people who do "nice" things. (The bland leading the bland and both falling into a "nice" rut.)

I'm sick of the literature that reduces the Christian life to quiet times, fixed grins, happy talk, and saccharine songs. I'm tired of writers and speakers who indulge our whimpering and whining, who prescribe endless therapy for problems we wouldn't have if we weren't so outrageously self-centered, who encourage us to feather our own already fairly comfortable nests while oohing and aahing over our inconveniences as if they were crucifixions.

I'm sick, too, of scholarly literature that pours scorn on the people of God, judging them as nothing but self-serving hypocrites who either worship themselves or a petrified faith that should have been discarded centuries ago. These wise men for whom, I suspect, life has become sour and boring, rip away the foundations of the Christian faith, leaving disciples unsure of who they are and what direction they should go. What has the appearance of bold scholarship has no upward call and no sure message. Rather, it's the bored and peevish ramblings of academics who have lost their way.

Finally, I'm one of a great multitude who are sick of themselves! But not so sick that we don't know who we are and whose we are. Not so sick that we can't see the glory of the biblical Christ, can't feel the magnetism of his person and the wholesome rebuke of his life, can't recognize our hunger for something more glorious as the work of God in us.

No, in spite of our human limitations, we see the Christ out in front of us, calling us onward and upward. We are determined, with blood-red earnestness, to live heroically for God and the world he so loves that he gave his Son.

The British literary historian Quiller Couch takes pleasure in telling us that during a certain time in Britain every writer in the nation wrote with one eye on a little island in the South Seas where Robert Louis Stevenson was living out his last days. They were hoping, he tells us, that perhaps Stevenson would somehow hear of what they had written and "not think too badly of it."

For something like two thousand years, millions of people have been living out their little lives with an eye on Jesus Christ, daring to wish that he might see their efforts to glorify him through a radiant life and hoping that he "might not think too badly of them."

I don't think they need to grind their bones in worry about it. It isn't hard to imagine Jesus getting to his feet in admiration when Stephen faced the mob; we can almost hear him shout an encouraging "Yes!" when one of his gloriously beats a temptation or rises from a bad fall to begin again.

What a Lord!

ONE

# COMPASSION

George Gissing was going along a road one day and he saw a poor little lad, maybe ten years old, crying bitterly. He had lost sixpence with which he had been sent to pay a debt. "Sixpence dropped by the wayside, and a whole family made wretched. I put my hand in my pocket, and wrought sixpenny-worth of miracle."

—J. H. Jowett

✦

# Dead at Thirty-Two

✦

When he saw the crowds, he had compassion
on them, because they were harassed and
helpless, like sheep without a shepherd.

—Matthew 9:36

About two hundred years ago (or was it yesterday?), Alice lived two doors away from us. She didn't profess to be a Christian, and those of us who knew her well knew she had struggles, like the rest of us, which she didn't always win. But Christ loved her. And, Christian or not, he worked in her life, making her cheerful, sensitive, sympathetic, and generous. Like so many others, she had a hard life. She had four children, serious heart trouble, and a hard-drinking husband who gave her many a beating.

I can still see her in the street, leaning against her window with her arms folded, wisecracking with the neighbors, milkman, or anyone who showed the slightest interest in being friendly. More than once I caught her crying, wondering how she was going to get through the week with so little money and so many things to be done with it. She was thin, too thin, and her skin was clear and smooth, almost transparent. (With skin like hers, we could easily see the bruises.) She kept her hair swept up, and her eyes were strikingly beautiful—pale blue and big and round. She died undergoing her second heart surgery. I think she was thirty-two years old.

Alice reminds me of all the people I've known who, day after day, *without end,* struggle to keep their heads above water. *Never,* in all their lives, are they able to go to a shop and buy something without first doing serious arithmetic. *Never,* from the cradle to the grave, are they sure the money for rent, heat, food, and clothing is going to be there. It's that endless grind that beats so many people, that takes the light out of their eyes. They march up from the gates of birth with sunshine on their faces, dreaming dreams, purposing purposes, but life just wears them down. Then we put them in the ground at the age of thirty-two, look at each other sadly, and shrug in helplessness.

It's at times like these that you hungrily search for moments when you did something comforting for the Alices in your life, something kind, something that brought a smile or a happy, speechless look of gratitude. Not so you can brag and think you weren't such a bad neighbor after all. No, it's just that it becomes important to know that people like Alice didn't die without a moment of knowing somebody cared, without friendly arms to hold them while they sobbed. It's at times like these that your heart remembers and is glad for all the moments when cups of sugar were loaned or borrowed or packets of tea were halved.

I'm sick and tired of comfortable Christians dismissing other people's heartache as if it made no difference in how those people respond to God. I'm tired of comfortable Christians receiving endless pulpit and book therapy because they have a "tough time," while people like Alice (who number in the multimillions) are given the take-it-or-leave-it kind of offer of the gospel.

Take me, for example. As well as I think I know what I'm talking about in this matter, as deeply as I think I feel about it, I still slip into the notion that we all have an equal shot at life. *That just isn't true!* But if I know it isn't true, how can I forget that so quickly and easily? Why do I look at people and assume that each of them has the same chance to hear and respond?

Didn't I hear that the people of Israel—beaten and despairing because of generations of exploitation and oppression—didn't I hear that when the Good News came, they weren't able to hear it because of their pain?[1] Their hard lives had beaten the hope out of them; their long, unchang-

**I still slip into the notion that we all have an equal shot at life.**

ing weeks and months and years made it too hard for them to believe. And God took all that into account!

Oh sweet Lord Jesus, what am I going to do about what I'm writing here? What are we who are reading this going to do? Can you not enter our lives with greater vision and enable us to see Alice all around us? Are we deliberately keeping you out? Are we afraid to see? We seem to be able to dismiss this whole matter with such ease. At least, *I* seem to be able to. I wish I could believe I am the only one, but I know I'm not.

Lord, have you been speaking to us all along, but because we have preferred to hear other things, you have decided to let us go our way? Don't leave us this way. It's so ugly, and we long for your beauty.

♦

# Show Him Your Hands

✦

The King will reply, "I tell you the truth, whatever you did for one of the least of these brothers
of mine, you did for me."
—Matthew 25:40

Mary was just a girl when she died. Both her parents died when she was a child, so it was up to
her to be mother to brothers and sisters. She worked too
hard, slept too little, ate poorly, and worried endlessly.
Over the years it all took its toll.

Just before she died, Mary was agitated and weepy. She
expressed concern about meeting Christ because she felt
she had nothing big and brave to offer him in gratitude
for his blessing her and the other children throughout her

short life. One of her brothers who was sitting on the bed stroking her thin, fevered fingers said, "You could show him your hands." I don't know what the young man's theology might have been or ultimately became; I do know, however, that he'd gotten to one of the centers of God's concern.

Mary's hands were old too soon. When they should have been making daisy chains, they were washing clothes; when they should have been pushing a swing in a playground, they were scrubbing floors and cooking meals.

I can't abide a religion that says none of this matters! I cannot hold to a religion that dismisses this kind of reality by immediately warning against "salvation by works" and continually reminding us of the need for "sound doctrine." For pity's sake, we all know that legalism is heresy.

I'm just like everyone else: there are truths I cannot deny and there are truths I will not hear attacked without rising to their defense (where it seems profitable). Truth matters! God has not required us to park our brains in order to please him; in fact, he has called us to engage our intellects as well as our passions. Tearjerking stories are no substitute for reasoned discourse; lies that tug on the heartstrings can never replace justified claims of truth. Someone greater than all of us said that truth frees. So I'm aware of the need for "propositional truth," but I'm ashamed when we "lovers of truth" love only the truth we tell, love especially the truths we hold distinctively, and glibly bypass spellbinding self-sacrifice with a, "Yes, but what do they *believe?*"

Truth is for doing! Theological truth enables us to live sacrificial lives. A little theology goes a long way when creatively applied. There's more to being an imitator of

God than holding correct views, and this is especially true when the views are hard to relate to genuine social concerns.

An old *Christianity Today* cartoon offers this: A man is sitting in a hotel room. His hair's a mess, his shirt is lying open, and his tie is loosed. He's unshaven, his eyes have deep, dark rings around them, and he has a look of desperation on his face as he hoarsely says into the phone, "Pastor, you've got to help me. I've lost my job, my wife has left me, the kids have gone with her, I'm in debt over my head, and I won't be able to pay the hotel bill. Please, tell me, is Revelation 20 literal or figurative?"

Philosophy professor Christina Sommers, in a lecture on ethics, tells a story from Saul Bellow's collection of traditional Jewish tales. In a small Jewish town in Russia, there is a rabbi who disappears each Friday morning for several hours. His devoted disciples boast that during those hours their rabbi goes up to heaven and talks to God. A stranger moves into town, and he's skeptical about all this, so he decides to check things out. He hides and watches. The rabbi gets up in the morning, says his prayers, and then dresses in peasant clothes. He grabs an axe, goes off into the woods, and cuts some firewood, which he then hauls to a shack on the outskirts of the village where an old woman and her sick son live. He leaves them the wood, enough for a week, and then sneaks back home. Having observed the rabbi's actions, the newcomer stays on in the village and becomes his disciple. And whenever he hears one of the villagers say, "On Friday morning our rabbi ascends all the way to heaven," the newcomer quietly adds, "If not higher."[1]

Christians will tell you there is another Jewish rabbi who really did ascend all the way to heaven and who would be thrilled at the behavior of the Russian rabbi. Of this rabbi, one of those who knew him best wrote, "He went about doing good and healing all that were oppressed by the devil, for God was with him."[2]

It is that Jewish rabbi, Jesus Christ, who claims that one day he will judge the world.[3] And on that Day one of his central concerns will be what we *did* with truth. Our destiny will hang on whether or not we cared for and catered to the needs of others. Maybe his first question won't be "What are your views on this or that issue?" but "Will you show me your hands?"

# Shiny Boots

✦

Do everything without complaining or arguing, so

that you may become blameless and pure,

children of God without fault in a crooked

and depraved generation, in which you

shine like stars in the universe.

—Philippians 2:15

Even Jesus had his quiet and restful moments of pleasure in the presence of his friends or in the solitude of an evening roaming the hills of Judea with his Father. So there's no need for us to be ashamed of taking some rest or enjoying the pleasures of life as gifts from God. We don't have to be heroes every moment of the day, doing extraordinary deeds and making history at every turn of our heels.

It's okay to be ordinary once in a while.

But while ordinary is beautiful, great people and great deeds color life, add depth and strength to it, cleanse it as a fresh sea breeze clears the air, and help us breathe free.

George Adam Smith, brilliant Old Testament scholar, commenting on Isaiah 32:2 and speaking of great people, offers this lovely and challenging piece:

> Great men are not the whole of life, but they are the condition of all the rest; if it were not for the big men, the little ones could scarcely live. . . . In the East . . . where the desert touches a river-valley or oasis, the sand is in a continual state of drift from the wind . . . which is the real cause of the barrenness of such portions of the desert at least as abut upon the fertile land. . . . But set down a rock on the sand, and see the difference its presence makes. After a few showers, to the leeward side of this some blades will spring up; if you have patience, you will see in time a garden. How has the boulder produced this? Simply by arresting the drift.
>
> Now this is exactly how great men benefit human life. A great man serves his generation, serves the whole race, by arresting the drift.[1]

I like that. I've seen it happen again and again. The weak among us who longed for "more" were overwhelmed by the drift of blinding forces and strength-sapping failures. Then someone came to us and sheltered us by their life. Protected from suffocating influences by their strong, cheerful stand, we were able to survive long enough to gain some strength of our own.

Listen, isn't this a stirring passage? "Each man will be like a shelter from the wind and a refuge from the storm, like streams of water in the desert and the shadow of a great rock in a thirsty land."[2]

Only the Christ is always like this, but those who have gladly given him their lives long and labor to be like him. They strive to protect people from criticism that's too hot and hard for them to bear, and they try to make it easier (if not easy) for wanderers to believe—not only in the goodness in others but in the possibility of goodness in themselves. By the grace of God, these compassionate souls reflect the life of Christ before the widening eyes of those who do not know him.

That's really what happened to one man, a former army sergeant, who had spent his whole adult life in the military. He and his buddies had all been "hard men," but none any harder than a corporal he had served with.

Astonishingly, the corporal announced he was giving his life to Christ, and as he was baptized, a new man arose. The transformation in his case was immediate and radical: no more booze, no more foul language, no more brawling, no more lascivious stories. A deeper reality now permeated his life.

At first the group of soldiers was amused, then skeptical, expecting a return to normal. Then, for a while, they were awed. But eventually, the hard men began to provoke the corporal. The insults mounted—jeers, bawdy songs, drunken truculence, and threats of violence. Vile jokes were deliberately told in his presence and for his benefit. Once in a while, he looked as though he might lose it and respond in kind—but he didn't. The sergeant was especially irritated—he just "knew" it wouldn't last.

One day the men returned from a long, tiring day's march, mud covered and bone weary. The sergeant pulled off his boots and collapsed on his cot. Attracted by the silence across the tent, he glanced over and saw the corporal down on his knees by his cot, praying. The sergeant was furious! He grabbed a muddy boot and flung it at the man, hitting him on the shoulder. The corporal continued to pray. Now the sergeant was incensed. He sat up on the cot, grabbed the other boot, and flung it hard at the praying man's head. It struck home, and the corporal grunted and rubbed his head—rubbed and rubbed . . . and prayed and prayed.

Later the sergeant wakened to find the corporal gone and his own filthy boots shined and polished, sitting by his cot. That, said the sergeant, was the last straw. That kind of heroism for Christ's sake turned him to God.

The corporal's kind of gallantry can make some of us too self-critical, leading us to think we're pretty well useless; but that would be a mistake. The most trying thing for soldiers in wartime, so they say, is the waiting, the staying in one place until some dramatic command is given or some critical action has begun.

Patient parents, respectful children, devoted families, cheerful and compassionate medical staff, honest laborers, loyal friends, sensitive and fair employers, honorable and eager employees—when they wait faithfully in the name of Christ, they make it easier for others to come to faith. A flash of brilliance is wonderful in a dark world, but a steady light is invaluable.

And yet, it won't hurt us to be moved by the exceptional. Exceptional deeds in otherwise lovely but ordinary lives change us. We cherish the sun's unbroken light three hundred and sixty-four days of the year, but we're still stunned by that eclipse.

# The Hero and Mrs. MacIntosh

✦

Finally, all of you, live in harmony with one
another; be sympathetic, love as brothers, be
compassionate and humble.

—1 Peter 3:8

T o feel wanted; to believe there's someone who'd be
deeply pained if you weren't there; to suppose,
most of the time, that you really make a difference; to
know tender moments when someone holds you; to feel
tender lips softly against your cheek; to hear whispers that
life would be so empty without you—to live without
these things is hardly to live at all! In a throwaway world,
it's easy for sensitive souls to feel like paper plates or plas-
tic forks.

Family members can make one another feel as if they're temporarily useful but ultimately dispensable. "I'm an unpaid servant in my own home," a woman sobbed. "All I'm good for is washing, cooking, and cleaning! A maid would suit them just as well." Or a family man says with a sigh, "They see me as the breadwinner, and that's all."

We all sorely want to be wanted as well as thought useful. It's a terrible blow to feel used and not wanted. Those who make us feel both are doing us a great service; they're saving our lives.

Jerry Harvill told a story about novelist Marjorie Byrd, who was visiting the MacIntosh home in the western Highlands of Scotland. A gale was howling around the cottage that lay outside the village, and Mr. MacIntosh was away on business. At the height of the fierce storm came a knock at the door. A family friend, a young lad, severely crippled and drenched to the skin, had walked from the village to check on Mrs. MacIntosh. She brought him in to warm at the fire.

**If you think that brightening up others' lives is too big a job, make up your mind to brighten their days!**

"Aren't you afraid?" the boy asked Mrs. McIntosh and her guest intensely.

The novelist was about to say no, when Mrs. MacIntosh spoke the words every boy longs to hear: "Of course we were afraid," she said, "but now that you're here, it's all right, because now we have a man in the house."

The boy straightened his twisted frame, looked at the two women, and said with a firm voice, "Well, then, I'd best be checking to make sure everything is snug."

Christians will tell you that Jesus Christ had this quality. Without being naive or unrealistic, he could look past the failures of the people he knew and gladly, warmly express his gratitude for what they gave to him.[1]

If you think that brightening up others' lives is too big a job, make up your mind to brighten their days! Make them feel they have something to offer, that they enrich your life; that, somehow, just knowing they're in this world with you makes the challenges and the heartaches easier to bear and the joys that much more joyous. Let them know they make a difference!

# Davie

✦

For God did not send his Son into the world

to condemn the world, but to save

the world through him.

—John 3:17

Davie was about eight years older than I was. To an eleven- or twelve-year-old kid, this well-dressed, charismatic, handsome guy was someone to be admired. He was a bit of a wild one, but we all grinned at much of his wildness. He was something of a hero to most of the kids I hung around with.

Davie had always dabbled with booze, but I began to notice him being drunk more and more often, and he started getting into street fights. Soon, Maggie, his fiancée, dropped him. He went down like a stone. I saw less and less of him. The next time I saw him, a few years later, he was a chronic alcoholic. He had gone from one hospital to the next and then into a hospital for the mentally unstable.

Just yesterday, as I was driving down a busy main street in Belfast, an old man ran right out in front of me. He was clutching a bottle in a brown paper bag, and his hair was as white as snow. I didn't hit him, but as he lurched away I looked into his face—it was Davie. Old too soon. And lost!

Not just lost in some narrow, religious sense—but lost to health, to self-respect, to Maggie, to his parents, to marriage, and to children. Gone were all of the possibilities of his manhood, lost were potential dreams, noble deeds, and noble thoughts. He was lost to friendship, lost to himself, and oh, sweet Lord, lost to you too. And somehow I feel responsible.

If you asked me how, I wouldn't be able to tell you. But the feeling's there. I feel a deep sense of personal loss, even though we were never personal friends. Is that why I feel responsible? Because we were never friends? Maybe all this is just foolishness, but somehow, I feel we've all suffered loss in the loss of Davie.

He must live in one of the multitude of hostels scattered throughout Belfast. I'm wondering if every now and then, he might sit alone in the dark, missing the Davie he once knew, wondering how he got into this shape, and wondering how in God's name he'll ever get out of it—or if he'll get out of it.

With Prince Charles' flight to Europe, thousands in Scotland saw their dream of self rule die, saw hopes smothered and glory missed. In the young prince's failure, they saw their own, and one of their poets sadly wrote:

> Sing me a song of a lad that is gone,
> Say, could that lad be I? . . .
> Give me again all that was there,
> Give me the sun that shone!
> Give me the eyes, give me the soul,
> Give me the lad that's gone . . .
> Billow and breeze, islands and seas,
> Mountains of rain and sun,
> All that was good, all that was fair,
> All that was me is gone.[1]

*Davie*

♦

I miss Davie, somehow. And when I think of all the other Davies who hang around your corners and mine, I can't completely rid myself of guilt feelings that I should be so blessed while others are so lost. I'm determined by the grace of God to do more than the little I'm doing to "justify" my having so much.

Ah, Davie, Davie.

# A Card around His Neck

✦

When Jesus saw this, he was indignant. He said to
them, "Let the little children come to me, and do
not hinder them, for the kingdom of God
belongs to such as these."
—Mark 10:14

Author C. S. Lewis confessed that he didn't especially enjoy the company of little children. This is
a bit surprising, but not to the discredit of that wonderful man. Francis Xavier, Catholic missionary and theologian, on the other hand, had a healthy obsession with
children. He worked a minimum of sixteen hours a day,
but more often he worked twenty. Once, when he was
exhausted, he went to his tent to rest for an hour, telling
those around him that he didn't want to be disturbed no

matter who asked for him. A few minutes later he rushed out of his tent and said, "I didn't mean a child. If it's a child, waken me immediately."

Both Lewis and Xavier knew that children were too important to be neglected. Too important even to leave the raising of them exclusively to their parents. Once children begin to spend more time at school and play than they do in the presence of their parents, there is a special need for nonfamily members to look after them. Mold a child, and you mold the world; sin against a child, and you sin against the world.

There's no change without ideas and truths, but ideas and truths come wrapped up in people. Relationships with people either redeem us or damn us, and it's comforting to know that the world outside our homes, while it has its dangers, contains good people who care for children who aren't their own.

Author L. A. Banks tells a lovely story of something that happened years ago on a journey across America. A pale, weepy little boy, riding on a train, is looking wistfully down the aisle where a mother and her laughing children are having something to eat. A man across from him notices his distress and asks him if he has nothing to eat. He says he has some food, but he isn't hungry. "I'm just a bit lonely," he admits. "There's lots of them over there," nodding at the happy clan, "and . . . they've got their mother."

"And you've lost yours, have you?"

"Yes," he says with quivering lip. And he is on his way to live with an uncle he's never seen. A lady from a town some way back had made him some sandwiches and had hung a card around his neck. She told him to show it to the ladies on the train, but he hadn't found the courage to do that yet. He tells the man he can read it if he wants to, and he pulls it around from inside his coat. It has his name and address on it, and below that it says, "Whosoever gives even a cup of cold water to one of these little ones, verily I say unto you, he shall in no wise lose his reward."

The man approaches the family on George's behalf, and before you know it, George has gentle arms around him and the woman's soothing voice is cooing, "poor, dear little fellow," and begging him to come with her to join her children.[1]

I love it when children meet adults who mean them no harm, who pity them in their vulnerability, and who go out of their way to make things easier as well as better. I love it when women, like that one on the train, take the trouble. George wasn't her child, so why should she bother? Because Mother Teresa was right: the world's greatest tragedy is unwantedness, the world's worst disease is loneliness. The man and woman on the train couldn't sit idly by and watch a child bear his pain alone; and while there was a limit to what they could do, they did what they could.

I read once about a teenage boy who found himself in terrible trouble. After his family threw him out, he landed in a foreign country where he made a go of it until somebody lied about him, and he landed in prison. He told the jailer he was innocent and that his family had mistreated him—the whole story. I don't know if the jailer believed his story or not. (I'm sure he'd heard his share of "bad luck" stories, of prisoners being "set up.") Anyway, he took the young man under his wing and treated him with extraordinary kindness. The boy grew up to become prime minister to the whole nation as well to save that whole part of the world from famine. The teenager's name was Joseph.[2]

Why did the jailer bother? Joseph wasn't his boy, and I'm sure he had plenty to worry about with a job as demanding as his. He did it for the same reason the people on the train helped young George. There are some people who just can't stand by and do nothing while children are enduring pain.

I hope that when my grandchildren—Jason, Cari, Erin, Alison, Kathleen, Alex, and Zachary—are in trouble and their loving parents aren't around, I hope they find the kind of people Joseph and George found.

# The Habit of Finding Fault

✦

Blessed are the merciful,

for they will be shown mercy.

—Matthew 5:7

A number of years ago, I told my older son, "Jim, I know I'm making mistakes along the way. I'm not always right, but I always have your welfare under consideration. Well, most of the time. This is my first shot at this adventure. I've never had a sixteen-year-old son before."

And then there was Linda. I made mistakes with her, too. But I had no practice runs. I had never been father to a fifteen-year-old girl. All of this was on-the-job training.

We parents mean well. We're selfish, impatient, demanding, and, at times, suffocating. But if we love our children, we wish them no injury and want only the best for them. As songwriter Paul Williams said, "Remember me, not for what I've done; but for the other things I always meant to do."[1]

Kids don't need parents who are indifferent—what a lonely world it is for a young person who feels that Mom or Dad is not interested. Nor do children need authoritarian parents who run the home like an army boot camp. Balance isn't easy to find. In part, that's because we want the best for our children; and if they haven't sense enough to see that, we can become irritated and act authoritarian.

Sometimes fathers catch a glimpse of themselves overdoing it, and it wrings from them the confession of Livingston Larned (I've adapted it a little):

> Listen, son, I'm saying this as you lie asleep, one hand crumpled under your cheek. I've stolen into your room alone. A few minutes ago, as I sat reading my paper, a stifling wave of remorse swept over me. I had been cross with you. I scolded you as you were dressing for school because you only dabbed your face with a towel. I chewed on you for not cleaning your shoes. I spoke angrily when you threw some things on the floor. I found fault at breakfast too. You spilled things, gulped your food, put your elbows on the table, put too much butter on your bread. As I left for work you waved and called, "Good-bye, Daddy!" and I told you to straighten your shoulders.
>
> The same thing in the afternoon. As I came up the road I saw you, down on your knees playing marbles. There were holes in your socks. I

humiliated you before your friends by marching you ahead of me to the house. Socks were expensive—"If you had to buy them, you'd be more careful." Imagine that from a father!

Do you remember, later, when I was reading my paper, how you came in, a bit timidly? I impatiently asked you, "What do you want?" You didn't say a thing. You threw your arms around my neck and kissed me. And you held me with an affection that God has set in your heart and which even neglect hasn't withered. Then you were gone, pattering upstairs to bed.

It was shortly after that that I felt the guilt and sickening fear. I've gotten into the habit of finding fault, regimenting, rebuking. This is my reward to you for being a boy! It wasn't that I didn't love you; it's that I expected too much of a boy. I was measuring you by the yardstick of my own years. But there is so much in you that is good and fine and true—like your enormous heart, which showed itself in your coming to kiss me goodnight in spite of everything.

Nothing else matters tonight, son. I'm here kneeling by your bed, ashamed. You wouldn't understand any of this if I told you about it. But tomorrow I'll be a real daddy. I'll be your chum, suffer when you suffer and laugh when you laugh. I'll bite my tongue when impatient words come. I'll keep saying, "He's nothing but a little boy—a little boy!"

I'm afraid I visualized you as a man. But looking at you now, crumpled and weary in your bed, I see you're only a little boy. Yesterday you were in your mother's arms. I've asked too much, too much.[2]

Is it just cheap talk to say, "If I had my life to live over again, I'd try harder to make Larned's confessional promise a part of my own practice"? How I wish I'd been a wiser lover—especially, but not exclusively, of my family. It seems I've spent so much of my life demanding too much, inspecting too much, like a spiritual Dick Tracy.

I'd do it differently if I had another chance. I'd make a positive and sustained attempt to use judicious praise rather than find fault, to warmly accept rather than critique. Most of the people I know up close need a break.

I think most of us ask too much.

# Bill the Peacemaker

✦

Do not judge,

or you too will be judged.

—Matthew 7:1

In 1891 a disagreeable student with a bitter tongue earned the name "Bill the Cynic." He wrote to a friend he had offended: "I know I am hard, proud, conceited, scornful, bitter . . . and insulting very often, and always selfish; but I don't like you to treat me as though I wasn't trying to do a bit better."

Now there's pain! Yes, I know Bill inflicted pain; I'm not trying to deny what everyone under the sun knew! I only wish to stress a point not often enough stressed.

(Well, it seems understressed to me.) Rebukers often get to enjoying the process. With something close to relish, they strip transgressors of their flesh, inch by inch, until they are a quivering mass of exposed nerve endings. The shock to the system is more severe than many can appreciate. It takes a long time to recover from harsh rebuke; some people never really do. Their potential for growth is blasted, and their life becomes one nervous recoil after another. The rebukers mercilessly strip them because "they must be made to see and feel the seriousness of their transgression."

It makes no sense at all to strip and traumatize and further shame those who give every indication that they're fully aware of their guilt. And how I detest the accusation, "She's only sorry because she got caught." What an ungodly thing to say when there's not a shred of evidence to substantiate it. What arrogance we show when we claim to be able to see behind heaving sobs and a burning face. God protect us from these clairvoyants who "know" the inner motivations of others!

**What arrogance we show when we claim to be able to see behind heaving sobs and a burning face.**

And it isn't unusual for the rebuker—when he warms to his work—to accuse the transgressor of additional wrongs and of callousness in connection with the original wrong. And a sad thing is, the transgressor is often afraid to protest these unjust accusations lest he be thought impenitent, lest doubt be cast on his sorrow over the matter in which he is truly guilty.

"Bill the Cynic" is actually a man called Edward "Bill" Wilson who accompanied Robert Scott to the Antarctic and to death. In March 1912, Scott wrote this of Wilson while they were both awaiting their end: "If this letter reaches you, Bill and I will have gone out together. We are very near it now; and I should like you to know how splendid he was at the end, everlastingly cheerful and ready to sacrifice himself for others." The expedition team called him "Bill the Peacemaker."[1] It was right in the early days to rebuke him when the occasion warranted it; it was wrong to treat him as though he "wasn't trying to do a bit better." The truth is, he'd been trying all along.

If you believe in a coming judgment, when all wrongs will be righted, there is added reason to do in meekness what must be done. For on that day, the one we meet won't be the dry-mouthed, spluttering punching bag we once rebuked. Rather, we'll meet his Champion—and He'll look strangely like all the guilt-ridden people we expertly butchered long ago.

# "Pretend You Know Me"

✦

Both the one who makes men holy and those who
are made holy are of the same family. So Jesus is
not ashamed to call them brothers.

—Hebrews 2:11

British preacher and author J. H. Jowett called Jesus
a "receiver of wrecks."[1] I love that. But there are
millions of people in each generation who live their lives
without getting involved in things that wreck their lives.
Not everyone is a "prodigal son" who has ended up in a
pigpen, eating slop. The return of a prodigal is a beautiful and joyous thing, but it makes no sense to say it is

more satisfying and lovely than a boy or a girl who never wallowed in shame and degeneracy. Jesus' Luke 15 parable shouldn't be understood to say otherwise.

It's finer and nobler that people resist the call of the "far country" and live in loving submission to God. It's true that we're all sinners and in need of forgiving grace (without exception), but it isn't true that we've all wallowed in moral filth to the extent that our lives became a sewer. And while it's true that God can make great use of those who've plumbed the depths of depravity and that the angels rejoice when his redeeming grace restores them to forgiveness and honorable living, we mustn't give the impression that to miss the pigpen is a disadvantage. Those of us who've wallowed in muck and led others to join us know what it means to look at the lives of gallant and honorable people and wish we had not been so wicked.

But having said all that, God's joy over moral wrecks who have been welcomed home is something to behold. More amazing is to recognize that someone as holy, as clean, and as noble as the Father of our Lord Jesus Christ welcomes them—with joy! This is precisely what offended one of Christianity's early critics, Celsus. He looked at these disciples of Christ and observed that they were all nobodies, ex-criminals, and slaves. There was hardly an honorable person among them. And as far as society viewed things, at least in Corinth, the famous apostle Paul saw it as Celsus saw it. He reminded the Corinthians that there were very few "big names" among them. Wasn't it John Bunyan who said he was glad that John 3:16 said "whosoever"? If it had said "John," he remarked, "I would have thought it was some other John; but since it said 'whosoever,' that let me in."

A story is told of an alcoholic who, though he lived with his other fellow victims of the booze industry on Skid Row, always insisted he had been a prominent businessman before he hit bottom. He smelled bad, looked bad, shook bad, and dressed bad, but he always told stories of better days—days when he was respected, wealthy, and had influential friends. His fellow alcoholics didn't believe a word he said. "You were always nothing, you're nothing now, and you'll always be nothing!" they told him—and this just unzipped him. The more they scorned him, the more he felt the need to tell his story.

One day while he was talking about his respectable past and they were mocking him, he saw an obviously successful man walking down the other side of the street. Desperation made him claim he knew the man, that they had been close in former years. That was a mistake, because his friends called him a liar and urged him to prove his story by approaching the stranger. What to do? He felt he had no option. He hurried across the road, and with great urgency he said quietly, "Please, mister, I'm sorry to bother you. I don't want any money, but please, will you pretend you know me? Please!"

> "Please, mister, I'm sorry to bother you. I don't want any money, but please, will you pretend you know me?"

A quick glance at the gawking friends told the man what had happened, and he sensed the desperation in the one before him. He let out a whoop, threw his arms around him, slapped his back, nearly shook his hand off his shoulder, and said (loud enough), "I haven't seen you in years. I wondered where you'd gotten to. How on earth are you managing?" He took him down the road, cleaned him up, got his hair cut, suited him up, fed him till he thought he'd burst, and put some money in his pocket. The rich man went on his way and the drunk back to Skid Row, but now he had substance for his stories. Someone had refused to be ashamed of him.

I know life is complex, and things aren't easily changed. I know simple acts of individual compassion and kindness don't change the whole of society. I know that simplistic approaches to pain and poverty can turn out to be "benevolent bungling." But I also know that it's too easy to convince ourselves that we shouldn't reach out and do crazy, compassionate acts.

Many of us are "too wise"; we see the complex issues too clearly and are able to critically appraise the pros and cons of acting on our feelings. Our appraisals are accurate, clinical, and sterile. We're never conned, never embarrassed by our enthusiasm, and we never feel sheepish or foolish for having acted passionately or spontaneously. We're everywhere known as the "prudent" ones who take our responsibilities seriously. In short, we are proper, deliberate, methodical, dispassionate—and barren.

But there is one who came, refusing to be ashamed of us. This one offers us not only a meal, clothes, a bath, and a temporary release, but he offers us his name, his permanent cleansing, and a permanent home—we need not go back to our personal Skid Row. And he makes this offer and bears the burden of this offer in the people who are his disciples. They are the instruments of his compassion and rescue. How could it be otherwise?

T W O

# COURAGE

Though love repine and reason chafe
There comes a voice without reply—
'Tis man's perdition to be safe,
When for the truth he ought to die.
                              —Ralph W. Emerson

✦

# "Merry Christmas, Father"

✦

Father, if you are willing, take this cup from
me; yet not my will, but yours be done.

—Luke 22:42

We can't forever stand in silence while the hearts of
our friends and neighbors are breaking. Our
behavior and theology must offer some comfort to people
in crisis. No, we don't have the definitive answers or the
complete cure for their ills; but the community of faith,
the followers of the crucified and risen Lord, must have
something to say and do when the "sore years" arrive.

The one thing we mustn't do is make promises in the name of the Lord that God hasn't given. A "health and wealth" gospel is no gospel at all. Its claim that a Christian's suffering is due to a lack of trust or commitment is a bold-faced lie. It isn't a lie only because it's untrue to the Scriptures; it's a lie because it's untrue to the experience of millions through the centuries who were devoted to God and his Christ.

Exemption from pain in life is not an option God offers his people. We never hear of the Christ apologizing to his disciples—"Look people, I'm sorry for getting you into all this trouble." The reverse is true: "Blessed are you when people insult you, persecute you, and falsely say all kinds of evil against you because of me."[1] Isn't that the kind of remark the apostle Peter is remembering when he says, "If you suffer as a Christian, do not be ashamed, but praise God that you bear that name"?[2] Peter assumes that heartache is part and parcel of being human, and sometimes, he says, it comes especially to those who bear the name of Christ.

Rather than apologizing for God, the Hebrew writer reminds his readers that their faith hasn't required them to shed blood—*yet*. "In your struggle against sin, you have not yet resisted to the point of shedding your blood."[3] He speaks as though shedding blood is fully expected of them, assuming they will do it when the time comes. And Peter, who rebuked Christ when he spoke of his cross[4]—that same Peter now tells his friends, "Dear friends, do not be surprised at the painful trial you are suffering, as though something strange were happening to you."[5]

Do you remember when Jeremiah complained to God, "You are always righteous, O Lord, when I bring a case before you. Yet I would speak with you about your justice."[6] He pours out his heart's complaint because he not only doesn't understand what God is up to, *he doesn't like it,* and he's hurting under the pressure. Do you remember God's response to him? He gave the poor man no answers or explanations—not even an immediate word of comfort. He said, "If you have raced with men on foot and they have worn you out, how can you compete with horses? If you stumble in safe country, how will you manage in the thickets by the Jordan?"[7]

I recognize that in all this, there are no "answers" offered to the problem of suffering. I'm simply taking note that this is the kind of world God's messengers moved in, and it never seemed to have entered their heads that it should be otherwise. Well, yes, when it came down to specific occasions and the hurt lay sore on their hearts, they asked for relief—and if it came, they praised God for it. They never thought it wrong to make requests to God for exemption or healing. But in the end, they never thought of saying anything but, "Nevertheless, not my will but thine be done."

I am not wishing to deny that Bible writers had questions about suffering. They did! From Job to Moses, from Joseph to Asaph, from Habakkuk to Jeremiah to Paul, men and women of faith have lifted their voices to God about it all. Still, though at times they felt that God had let them down they stayed at their posts while they waited to hear what he would say in response to their complaint.[8] They didn't quit! They knew there were complexities, matters beyond their understanding, and while they hotly protested God's refusal to deal with things that were obviously awry, their experience with him—not just individual experiences, but collective—taught them they ought to trust him, even while the questions remained unanswered. In the end, for all their human longings, they gallantly accepted the fact that he wouldn't exempt them from hardship.

I know it's a terrible thing to confess, but I have some dear friends whom I am reluctant to share . . . well, that's not quite what I'm wanting to say. I'm glad they have other friends, but I don't want their other friends to be as special to them as I am. That they feel toward others as deeply as they feel toward me seems to diminish me, to take something from me. I know it's nonsense. More than that, I know it's selfish of me, and in my better moments I renounce it for what it is. But there's that flaw in me that results in my wanting to monopolize their warmth and intimacy. I'm afraid they might care for others in such a way that I would lose a special place in their lives, don't you see?

I'm sure there's something of that spirit in my relationship with God, even though I know he's capable of loving everyone without anyone losing out. Just the same, sometimes, when things are a little harder to handle than usual, I can't help feeling that since I'm God's child, I should get special treatment.

It's hard for us "decent people" (which often includes non-Christians) to understand why we don't get privileged treatment from God. Rather than offering a list of explanations, let me share something that helped me understand my feelings better and that made me willing to think the thing through more patiently.

In the movie *Glory,* the son of a wealthy and prominent abolitionist is commissioned to head up the first black regiment of the Union army. His first volunteer is Thomas, his lifelong friend. Thomas is Afro-American, free, well educated, well spoken, refined, and well thought of; but when he enlists, he becomes a private, and his lifelong friend becomes his superior officer. Because they've enjoyed this wonderful relationship through the years, Thomas can't help but expect special treatment. Instead, he finds himself isolated from his friend. Private moments cease completely, personal conversation no longer exists, and all expressions of affection are suppressed.

The master sergeant gives Thomas an especially tough time precisely because he is the colonel's dear friend— and the colonel has to endure it, even though it breaks his heart. In one scene, the master sergeant again humiliates and injures Thomas, and the sensitive young black man goes to his old friend and sobbingly pleads, "Robert, I'd like to speak to you for a moment in private, if I may." But the colonel reminds him that he must go through channels if he is to speak to his superior officer. "Do you understand that, private?" he asks, and then he walks away.

From a place of warm privilege where he was known and loved, Thomas is decisively pushed back into the mass of other black volunteers. The other soldiers, dirt poor and strangers to comforts, had never known such privilege and so didn't miss the smiles, the warmth, the hugs, and the moments of intimacy. For Thomas, however, the special relationship is now a source of awful pain. Surely the colonel can't treat him as though he had never known him? What harm can be done by maintaining their beautiful, warm friendship? How can he pretend that Thomas is no different than all these strangers? And so Thomas's pain is worse than the pain of all those who never had Colonel Robert G. Shaw as a friend. Thomas's

◆

pain was not due to the fact that the colonel was making a difference between him and the other troops, it was because he *wasn't* making a difference—that's what crushed him.

But as the story unfolds, Thomas comes to terms with what he knows in his heart needs to be done. He sorrowfully surrenders his intimacy with the colonel for the welfare of all the other volunteers with whom he now develops a new sense of brotherhood. The early Thomas was noble and honorable; the later Thomas was even nobler.

On Christmas Eve, the colonel is walking alone between the tents, feeling lonely. He and Thomas meet by accident—both lonely and in pain. The enlisted man, speaking with difficulty, says, "Robert, I just wanted to say . . . I just wanted to say . . ." and then, unable to finish what he started, he says quietly with a sad little smile, "Merry Christmas, Robert."

**Maybe if we carry our heartache well, doors will open so we can tell the Story of one who bore all our pain in his own body.**

Perhaps we should recognize that there's something more important than getting special treatment from a God who is our friend. However hard it might be for us to step back and take our place among all the other "enlisted" people, this is what Thomas calls us to.

Maybe it's important for us to carry our trouble hopefully, so that others, even the jeering ones, might be led to ask how we can hope in the face of our pain. Maybe if we carry our heartache well, doors will open so we can tell the Story of one who bore all our pain in his own body.[9]

Maybe while there is a child anywhere in the world who is subjected to pain; maybe while there is a man or woman who has to wrestle with humiliation, hunger, and injustice; maybe as long as any of that goes on, we won't get special treatment. But while any of that is going on, maybe we shouldn't *want* special treatment. Maybe that's something of what the incarnation and Gethsemane's "nevertheless" means. Maybe that's what "Eloi, Eloi, Lama Sabacthani?" means.

Maybe sometimes—when we're about to pour out a string of requests to a God we think should give us preferential treatment—maybe sometimes we should forget the list and simply say, "Merry Christmas, Father."

♦

# I Will Do More Than Live

✦

Be on your guard; stand firm in the faith;

be men of courage; be strong.

—1 Corinthians 16:13

I t would appear that some people just insist on being on the whining side rather than the winning side. Every time they open their mouths, it's a bleating session. You'd think the Bible had said, "Blessed are the moaners."

*Blessed are They That moan*

Most of us don't really complain about people complaining. We all know life can be tough. It's the *whining* that sets us on edge. I must be careful here not to confuse genuine and prolonged suffering with once-in-a-while pain, but I must also trust the reader to know when he or she has met up with one or the other. In every city of the world, in every age, you come across or read about people who have looked suffering right in the eye and refused to buckle under.

Yvonne and Yvette are thirty-two years old and permanently joined at the head. They have two independent brains, but they share one bloodstream. They get on with living.

Mark Hicks could turn his head only thirty degrees. That's all the control he had of his body. But he became a brilliant painter, and the movie about his life, *Gravity Is My Enemy,* won an Oscar in 1981.

Terry Fox, a twenty-two-year-old Canadian who contracted bone cancer, ran the eighteen hundred miles between Saint John's and Thunder Bay with one artificial leg to raise money for cancer research.

Then there was Helen Keller and Annie Sullivan.

And there was David Livingstone, the famous explorer of Africa, who at ten years of age, studied from six in the morning to eight at night. By the time he was eighteen, he had so mastered Latin that he could read Horace and Virgil with ease.

The atheist Sigmund Freud lived in constant pain the last sixteen years of his life and endured thirty-three operations. But he stuck to his work to the very end.

A friend of U.S. Senate Chaplain Lloyd Ogilvie had lost all vitality and enthusiasm and had become boringly negative. Ogilvie confronted him about it and assured him that he now had a choice between degenerating into the grave or living. Weeks later he received a letter of six words: "Dear Lloyd, I've decided to live."[1]

This is a tricky area, and before we crush everyone with a verbal backhander, we need to know the facts. If

it's a friend, we will search the matter out. If plain talk is
what is needed, we will speak it.

Sometimes we just have to make up our minds to live.
William Ward sounded a call that stirs the blood:

> I will do more than belong—I will participate.
> I will do more than care—I will help.
> I will do more than believe—I will practice.
> I will do more than be fair—I will be kind.
> I will do more than forgive—I will forget.
> I will do more than dream—I will work.
> I will do more than teach—I will inspire.
> I will do more than earn—I will enrich.
> I will do more than give—I will serve.
> I will do more than live—I will grow.
> I will do more than be friendly—I will be a
> friend.

# A Little Something Extra

✦

The Lord is my shepherd,

I shall not be in want.

—Psalm 23:1

S ammy Law and his wife, Jean, lived out in the sticks, not far from Coleraine. He had seen combat close up in Korea, and were it not for some comrades, he would have gotten more than a bullet in the foot. Jean was a hospitable soul, and like so many other country women, she could bake the most delicious bread. Smother it with butter as it came straight from the griddle, and a king couldn't eat better. It was Sammy who took me fishing for the very first time in my life.

I spent the night with the Laws, talking into the later hours (as usual). I had barely shut my eyes when Sammy shook me awake to go fishing. It was 4:30 in the morning. I didn't know such an ungodly hour existed until that moment. It was cold, wet, windy, and dark as we made our way to the river. As I shivered, I wondered if I were quite right in the head; but it was too late to debate the wisdom of the venture.

Sammy put a worm on my hook, threw the line out into the dark river, and moved off into the shadows downriver. In the early morning quietness, I could hear him humming now and then, and I could hear the swish of his line as he repeatedly cast it into the river. I was miserable, and the worm on my line wasn't even trying.

I don't know how long I stood there, wishing I were back in bed or at least somewhere comfortable, before I felt it. A fish was nibbling on the worm at the end of the line, and I felt his nibble come up through the line, into my hands, and from there to somewhere behind my bellybutton. Down there in the dark, beyond my vision, there was life, tugging on my line. He ate up all my worm and then took off. The safest meal he ever had, no doubt. But he had made contact with me, and that magic moment has stuck with me now for more than thirty years. I reeled in my line, checked to make sure the worm was gone, groped my way down to Sammy, and had him put another worm on the hook. Then back I went in search of more adventure.

I don't remember anything else about that trip, but with startling clarity I can recall how I felt *before* that fish mugged me for my worm and how I felt *after* he made his hit. Out of the darkness, when I least expected it, when I might have been tempted to think there was nothing there, a gentle tugging told me I was in touch with life—and misery became excitement. For those who've fished all their lives and have caught about eleven and a half million trout, this may be old hat; but it was a magical experience for me.

Now I know this doesn't rank as a theological "argument," and I know, too, that it will make no sense to those who do not share my Christian faith; but I think God watches us and knows that sometimes our poor little minds wander, our faith falters, and the pressures of life weigh so heavily on us that we need *something more.* My sister Margaret put it this way (and I know she was right): "Sometimes we're in special need of him. He knows this, and he gives us 'a little something extra.' "

When we're miserable and really wondering what it's all about, God gives a little tug on our line to let us know we are dealing with life when we deal with him—that we aren't just shivering alone in the dark. His tug might be a remarkable answer to prayer, an incredible "coincidence," or an experience so uplifting we can't do anything but look up and say thank you.

And I want you to know, I'm not talking about God getting people parking spaces that save them a ninety-second walk or God leading people to the right hairdresser. I'm talking about how he makes his presence known in times of inner stress, of loneliness, of weariness. I'm talking about times when life is

> When we're miserable and really wondering what it's all about, God gives a little tug on our line to let us know that we aren't just shivering alone in the dark.

pressing down on you, when your heart's breaking, when people are being mean and your soul needs a little something extra. Just when you need it, there's an arm around your shoulder, someone strokes your hair, a letter comes out of the blue, a loved one recovers from illness, a phone call cheers you, a whispered and genuine apology makes the sun shine again, a fear finally dissolves. All are tugs on the line—God letting you know he's around. That little something extra enables you to press on joyfully. Or if not filled with joy, at least, helped by the knowledge that you are seen and cared for.

And for you who are burdened with pain you haven't sought and for you who haven't yet experienced that little something extra—continue to be brave and strong and live without it. Trust him still. And maybe when the ultimate day arrives, you who were gallant enough to live without the tug will receive a little something extra for being so brave.

# Captain Freedom

✦

The weapons we fight with are not the weapons
of the world. On the contrary, they have divine
power to demolish strongholds.

—2 Corinthians 10:4

D o you remember Captain Freedom from the *Hill
Street Blues* television series? He was the amateur
crime-fighter who wore circus tights, a cape, WWI flying
helmet, goggles, and trainers. He felt called to fight
against evil. He carried no weapons—all he had was his
physical presence, his words, and his innocence.

During a shootout with the police, armed robbers
fatally shot him dead when he jumped up on a car and,
with his arms raised, shouted, "Stop this criminal act!" It

was only a dumb television show, but it held magic for me; I couldn't get Captain Freedom out of my mind for days. The purity of his intentions, his fearless innocence, the way he risked himself, his vulnerability—they drew me to the character. Society would call him a "nut"; and in a world of practical and cynical people, nuts have nothing to offer.

And yet, Captain Freedom was a nut on the good side. Crazy little people who lay their lives on the line get in close to our hearts. Some even grab sufficient headlines to inspire others who turn them into Don Quixotes about whom they write and sing songs. The cautious and deliberate among us, the "Let's think this through, now" types, aren't the kind they write books or ballads about. We couldn't be more tame or more boring.

When the United Kingdom was about to explode its first hydrogen bomb in the Pacific, the churches wrung their hands and held emergency meetings. But one quiet little preacher, sixty years old, withdrew all his savings, bought a boat, and sailed right into the targeted area. After dealing with the inconvenience, Britain went on to complete the nuclear test. The little man accomplished nothing, we say. Oh, I don't know. He still tugs at our conscience more than forty years later.

Meanwhile, the good news is that Captain Freedom is alive and well in the people who renounce all the warring ways to bring peace, all the evil ways to make society better, all the filthy ways to make us clean, and all the enslaving ways to make us free.

So here's to you who continue the battle against evil, even when you aren't convinced that your little gesture will make much difference. Here's to you who lay your reputations on the line, risking the sneers and put-downs.

Here's to you who confront evil, taking it on with no weapons other than those with which Jesus Christ faced his judgment at Golgotha. Let them sneer and say you're a fool. Long after what's-his-name has been fully forgotten, someone will speak your name in grudging admiration.

Weary Matthew Arnold, English poet and critic of religion, wrote this sad but strangely inspiring poem:

> Creep into thy narrow bed,
> Creep, and let no more be said!
> Vain thy onset! all stands fast;
> Thou thyself must break at last.
>
> Let the long contention cease!
> Geese are swans and swans are geese.
> Let them have it how they will!
> Thou art tired; best be still!
>
> They out-talk'd thee, hissed thee, tore thee.
> Better men fared thus before thee;
> Fired their ringing shot and pass'd,
> Hotly charged—and broke at last.
>
> Charge once more, then, and be dumb!
> Let the victors, when they come,
> When the forts of folly fall,
> Find thy body by the wall.[1]

# The Belfast Ropeworks

✦

For God did not give us a spirit of timidity, but a
spirit of power, of love and of self-discipline.
—2 Timothy 1:7

I was twenty-one years of age (going on nine) when I
worked in the Ropeworks. At our end of the huge
shed, we produced big rolls of string; the six women who
tended the front end of the six big machines were "piece
workers"—the more string they made, the more money
they earned. I worked at the back of the machines, and
my job was to see that they were supplied with the raw
materials which came to me in large bins.

67

Sometimes the people supplying me were slow in getting the materials to me, and that meant the women had to wait until the supply came—and that meant less money. The rule was, whoever ran out of materials first was the first to get the fresh supply. Five of the women lived by that rule, but one of them completely ignored it. She would come around the back, check everyone else's supply, and compare it with her own. If she saw it was to her advantage to stop first and get the first fresh supply (thus avoiding having to join a line of waiters with perhaps four in front of her), she'd simply scrap the little she had left and say she had run out of material.

This was a sly way to jump to the front of the line— she was cheating. What was particularly bad was that she knew I knew she did it, and she'd look straight at me as though challenging me to say something about it. What was worse, the five other women knew I knew, and they knew I was doing nothing about it. They didn't say anything, but they often came round the back when she was cheating and, with a glance, let me know what they knew.

I felt terrible about it. Why didn't I stop her? I was afraid of her! She had a hostile look and a sharp tongue that could have opened a tin of salmon. I couldn't get up the nerve to face her. Not only was I guilt ridden, I was miserable because my gutlessness was apparent to all those women.

I don't know what it was that morning when freedom finally came. I vaguely recall having a marked difference of opinion with my wife, and maybe I came into work already heated up and with adrenaline flowing. We weren't long into the morning when the cheater came round the back for "business as usual," but I shouted down the room to her, "You can leave it as it is; you'll wait your turn like everyone else!" Well, she began to curse me and rant and rave, but she was too late—her doormat had tasted freedom!

I've never been what you'd call a brave person (though I've done a few little things in my life that I'd rank as brave), but this was *triumph*. I felt like Rocky. I was ecstatic; I felt like running, jumping, shouting. I wanted to go round to the front of the machines and tell all those women what I had done.

The depth of my elation embarrasses me now, since it was such a tiny incident—the kind of thing tens of thousands of people are doing at least once a day without a second thought. But it was liberation, don't you see. I had shaken off the chains of fear that woman had bound me with—the chains I had allowed her to bind me with—and now it was as if I could breathe deeply. I felt bigger, taller, more handsome, smarter—as though I owed nobody anything, as though my life had been given a fresh new start.

I know I was a better person for the next several days, living on the grand feeling, the inspiration of one noble deed, which for me, in my little fear-filled life, was brave. And, maybe, I'm still a stronger, finer person in some small way because I did what was right on that occasion. I like to think I am, though I'm not yet free of cowardice.

Whether any of that is true, this is true: I did what was right and what was needed and what was long overdue;

> She began to curse me and rant and rave, but she was too late—her doormat had tasted freedom!

and even now, when I rehearse the story in my mind, I feel my heart stir in a deep longing to be like that always.

Now, who do you need to kindly but plainly confront so you might enjoy some freedom and peace? Who is depending on you to obtain justice for them? Who do you need to face in order to deliver justice to those who depend on you? And how are you preparing to go about it?

♦

# "Your Friend, Herbie"

✦

The world was not worthy of them.
They wandered in deserts and mountains,
and in caves and holes in the ground.
—Hebrews 11:38

I heard a story of a seven-year-old boy who began his morning by falling off the school bus, cutting his head, and needing a couple of stitches. In the break between classes, he collided with another little boy. The result? A couple of loose teeth and a split lip. During the afternoon he fell and injured his arm, so Mr. Chapman, the school principal, thought they'd better get him home before anything else happened to him.

While driving him home, the principal noticed the boy was clutching something in his hand and he asked, "What do you have there?" The boy, all smiles, showed him a shiny quarter. "Where did you get it?" the man asked. The child said he found it on the playground, then he beamed with excitement and pleasure and added, "You know, Mr. Chapman, I've never found a quarter before. This is my lucky day!"

Don't you love that? A cut head, loose teeth, an injured arm, and a split lip—"my lucky day."

That's the kind of stuff heroes are made of. Heroes are people who find reason to rejoice in the midst of their pain, who refuse to be victims. They aren't fools—they don't deny the pain in life; they just won't let it be their lord and master. They refuse to gaze endlessly at their troubles until excessive self-pity takes over and ruins them completely. (There is some suffering, so deep, so stark, for which words like mine are virtual obscenities. I'm not addressing suffering of that magnitude.)

Now I don't want to make anybody feel guilty about feeling hurt and taking it seriously. I just wish I could say something that would enable those people to get up and go on, with their eyes on the good things of life as well as the evil, with their focus on the pleasant and joy-bringing aspects of life as well as the crushing experiences.

> **Heroes don't deny the pain in life; they just won't let it be their lord and master.**

Do you remember poor Miss Haversham in *Great Expectations?* Jilted on her wedding day, she lived the rest of her life in her wedding dress in the very room where she was when she received the news. The clocks were stopped at that very hour and remained precisely as they were when the awful news came. She died years before her death by fire finally came.

And then there's the heroine's father in *A Tale of Two Cities*. After spending years in the dreaded Bastille prison, he was brought to England and freedom. But late in the night they would often hear him do what he had been forced to do for years in the darkness of his cell: mend shoes and mumble his prison number when someone spoke to him. He had never been freed—they only moved his body from France to England.

Pain can crush and brutalize—it isn't always strengthening or character building. But the kind of pain that most of us face—real and sharp and sometimes prolonged though it is—can be overcome.

In real life, people like Viktor Frankl, who suffered terrible "medical experiments" under the Nazis in their evil camps, have taught us that it isn't what happens to us that ultimately matters but what we do with what happens to us. Glib? Coming from Frankl? Hardly. It's amazing how often one comes across suffering of the horrendous kind only to discover that the sufferer is ablaze with cheerful stubbornness!

You've seen the news coverage yourself—a refugee camp overrun with sickness and hunger, with death in every other hut. And then you see some smiling man or woman who looks all those challenges right in the eye and lives in spite of them. While rubbing shoulders with weeping, despairing, beaten people (and I have *no* criticisms to make of those people), such a person remains unbowed.

*"Your Friend, Herbie"*

♦

73

We need such brave spirits to change the world . . . all right, to change communities or individuals, if not the world. We need people who are realists—who acknowledge pain, their own included—but people who refuse to be intimidated into paralysis. Out of the pained masses come the suffering, intelligent, realistic souls who won't grovel. And all around the world, you come across people who choose to live and die in these conditions so they can ease the burdens of the other sufferers.

In a book called *Children's Prayers,* one of the children surveyed the challenges and risks that a life of faith in God can bring and wrote God a note that said, "Dear God, count me in. Your friend, Herbie."

# One More Time

✦

Bernard told me about an incident in his childhood. The boys would gather around each lunchtime to "chin the bar," with their girlfriends looking on proudly. The champ could pull his chin over the overhead bar ten times. Little Kenny was doing well if he managed seven. One day, said Bernard, Kenny did seven and tried for eight! Painfully, he managed it, and still held on. The little crowd was astonished as Kenny dragged his tortured body up for still another. Now he hung, unable to go up again but unwilling to let go. The group stood hushed, the champ was nervous, but Kenny looked beaten. Then the familiar voice of his sister rang out from the back: "Okay, now, Kenny, one more time!" That did it! Up he went, almost rupturing, but he matched the record.

When we're sorely tempted to stop trying in our marriage, we need someone to strengthen us with, "One more time!" When in business it begins to look as if "good guys finish last," we need an inner voice to challenge us with, "One more time!" When the pain and loneliness has been with us so long that we feel we just can't go on living another day, how we need someone to slip an arm around us and say, "Come on, now, one more time." When the evil habit seems all-powerful and we're tired of the relentless struggle, when we're on the verge of letting ourselves drift with the current, we must have someone to keep us going with, "Okay, now, just one more try."

**We can't always change a person's _circumstances_, but it is possible to change the _person_ so he or she can cope with the circumstances.**

She lived up the street from us. She was young, had three children (or was it four?), but no husband. We had her over a time or two, and she and my daughter, Linda, seemed to get on quite well. Frequently, we'd stop and talk with her briefly on the street—she was always quiet and pleasant. Yes, she said, she would like to visit with us again very soon. We didn't see her for quite a while, and then my wife, Ethel, asked a neighbor about her. "Oh, didn't you know?" the neighbor said. "She took her life."

She'd been hanging on by her fingertips. She couldn't try anymore, so she took pills to ease her way out of the painful, lonely world. How we wish we could now say in a practical way, "Come on, now, one more day"—but it's too late.

I'm not saying we should be all-knowing. That isn't possible. But we can develop a deeper sensitivity and eagerness to help where we can. We can't always change a person's *circumstances,* but it is possible—by "being there" with looks, words, and little kindnesses—to change the *person* so he or she can cope with the circumstances.

Even though we've failed in this so often and allowed opportunities to slip away, we mustn't retire from the game. We must find within us the voice of Kenny's little sister: "All right, now, one more time."

Rede

mption

# REDEMPTION

Dean Hole's great passion was the growing of roses. When his wife had visitors he used to sit silently till tea was over and then would say: "I should like you to come into my garden and see my roses." On one occasion a very beautiful girl was amongst the visitors. Dean Hole gazed at her for a long time, and then said to her, "Will you come into my garden? I should like my roses to see you."

—James Burns

✦

# The Candlesticks

✦

In the same way, let your light shine before
men, that they may see your good deeds and
praise your Father in heaven.

—Matthew 5:16

He was twenty-seven, a hard-working and illiterate
peasant who picked fruit for a living. The pay was
pathetic, but it was a job. He lived with his sister and her
seven children, and when winter came, he had no work
and the family had literally nothing to eat.

He endured their pain until he could endure it no
longer. Finally he broke the window of a baker's shop and
stole a loaf of bread. He was spotted! In the chase he
threw the loaf away but the cut on his arm proved him

guilty and the court gave him five years hard labor. He pleaded and protested (five years hard labor for stealing a loaf?) but it made no difference. With chains on his ankles, and a metal collar around his neck he was carted off to slavery.

In days when despair overwhelmed him, his fellow-prisoners would see his lips move soundlessly while he wept, and they'd see his raised right hand drop in stages as though he were laying his hand on heads of unequal height. The children! He'd done it for the children. A loaf, for pity's sake—it was only a loaf!

Four times he tried to escape from prison, but he only succeeded in adding years to his term. When they finally set him free, he had served nineteen years. Nineteen years to harbor deep bitterness, nineteen years to feed his anger, nineteen years—long enough to be dehumanized, to want to vent his spite against everyone around him, to hate and expect to be hated.

They gave him a yellow card which he had to show to law-abiding citizens. It meant he was a convict, newly released, on probation, and on his way to a town chosen for him by the authorities. When he came to the town, he was rejected by the innkeepers, despite his willingness to pay for food and lodging. Not even a barn was open to him. He was even driven from a kennel by a huge dog, and he found himself trying to sleep in the open, in the rain, on a wooden bench. Nineteen years in prison and now this!

"Have you knocked on that door?" a kind lady asked him. No he hadn't, but he would, he said, and he did. The door was opened and before anyone could reject him, the miserable and desperate man thundered out his name and the fact that he was a convict and almost challenged anyone to reject his pleading for food and rest. He wasn't aware that he had come to the house of a bishop. The bishop, who lived in utter simplicity, without grandeur or luxury, invited him in to the fire, urged the women who tended the residence to make him welcome and set the table for supper. The visitor suddenly realized he was dealing with a priest. "Ah, you're a priest. I saw a bishop once . . ." he babbled on and described the fine clothing of the bishop. The old priest kept calling him "mister" in that respectful way, and Jean (John) Valjean was warmed by this unfamiliar treatment.

Supper (a simple but substantial meal) was served on silver plates, and Valjean ate his fill. The ladies retired to bed, the old man went to pray and meditate, and the exhausted visitor collapsed on the warm bed to sleep. A good while before dawn the ex-convict entered the old man's room prepared to injure or kill him and steal the silver cutlery and plates. The sight of the trustful priest in peaceful sleep kept Valjean from the mad violence, but he gathered the silver together, climbed the garden wall, and went on his way.

**"You no longer belong to what is evil but to what is good. I have bought your soul to save it from black perdition, and I give it to God."**

The next morning the theft was discovered and a little later three policemen caught Valjean, and dragged him before the priest. They addressed the old man as "Monseigneur" and "his lordship the Bishop." The stupefied Valjean heard the old man say to him: "So here you are! I'm delighted to see you. Had you forgotten that

I gave you the candlesticks as well? They're silver like the rest, and worth a good two hundred francs. Did you forget to take them?" The astonished policemen left, and the bishop, gently and deliberately, said to the ex-con: "Jean Valjean, my brother, you no longer belong to what is evil but to what is good. I have bought your soul to save it from black perdition, and I give it to God."

You recognize, of course, the storyline of the incredible *Les Miserables* by Victor Hugo. I love the compassion of the old bishop and the consequent transformation of the brutal ex-convict into a man of tenderness, compassion, and selflessness. In this story, as so often in life itself, this kind compassion turned the world of the wrongdoer upside down; it wouldn't let him continue as he was; it melted his icy heart and gave him inspiration and strength to live a redemptive life—to make life better and stronger for others battling against the darkness that threatened to swallow them up. From that point on, the candlesticks were kept in a prominent place and became the symbol of the compassion shown to Valjean—the voiceless reminder of the debt he owed to all fellow-strugglers.

To do what is right and kind and brave is what God calls us to. This we should do no matter the results. But there's no way of knowing how such behavior alters the world for a person who is badly in need of such a vision. When a life has been filled with pain and injustice, with brutality and callousness, darkness invades the soul. It becomes difficult or almost impossible for the heart to believe there is any other reality. The old bishop's incredible kindness stood up and, in the name of God, defied the supremacy of darkness in the young man's life. Valjean's world changed and his eyes were opened, never to be closed again.

Scripture calls us, again and again, to do the right thing—the loving and redemptive thing—even in the face of criticism and injustice. You who are having a tough time are called to teach the rest of us what the Scriptures mean and how they are to be faced. You, more than the theologians and preachers, are the true interpreters. In you we see the texts confronted by brave and glorious hearts, and suddenly the written Word of God becomes more clear because, in you, the Word of God has become flesh again.

# Of Mothers and Grandmothers

✦

I have been reminded of your sincere faith,

which first lived in your grandmother Lois

and in your mother Eunice and,

I am persuaded, now lives in you also.

—2 Timothy 1:5

How many sights do you know that are lovelier than a fully grown man tenderly taking his elderly mother's arm and supporting her as she walks from the car to the door or from the waiting room to the doctor's examining room? Have you seen anything warmer than a grandmother reading a story to a child who sits transfixed or lies in peace or giggles like mad on her lap? Young mothers are beautiful, but what is it about a white-haired, elderly mother who still tenderly touches her fifty-year-old son and fixes his hair down as she did all those years ago when he couldn't do it for himself?

B. G. White of Jacksonville, Florida wasn't eavesdropping but was glad she heard what she heard. It was mid-October, and the trees along the Blue Ridge Parkway were ablaze with color. At an overlook where all this could be appreciated, she stood next to a woman who was showing the view to her elderly mother.

"Isn't it wonderful of God to take something just before it dies and make it so beautiful?" the daughter said as she gazed at the fallen leaves. "Wouldn't it be nice," the mother mused, "if he did that with people?" The younger woman looked at the stooped, white-haired figure beside her and said so softly that she thought no one else heard: "Sometimes he does."

I know that civilized societies and countries are held together by governments that seek the welfare of the law-abiding majority. I know that and I'm grateful for it. I also know that society is blessed by devoted school teachers, conscientious social workers, just judges, and ethical lawyers. I've seen what passionate men and women can do for societies when they embody noble principles in the centers of power. And only a fool can dismiss as nothing the thousands of community organizations in the cities and towns of the world that cater to the emotional and physical needs of countless unfortunate people. But all these beautiful men and women had mothers and grandmothers (or those who stood in the

> "Isn't it wonderful of God to take something just before it dies and make it so beautiful?"

place of mothers and grandmothers) who helped to shape their characters. For good or evil, it's people who change people—and there are no people who change people more than mothers and grandmothers!

One little boy put it very well when asked what a grandmother was. He said: "A grandmother is a lady who has no children of her own, so she loves everybody else's. Grandmas don't have anything to do except be there. If they take you for a walk, they slow down past leaves and caterpillars. They never say 'hurry up.' Usually they're fat, but not too fat to tie your shoes. They wear glasses, and sometimes they can take their teeth out. They can answer questions like why dogs hate cats and why God isn't married. When they read to you, they don't skip words or mind if it's the same story again. Everyone should try to have a grandmother, especially if they don't have television, because grandmas are the only grownups who always have time for you."

Mothers and grandmothers have been praised since the world began. One of the most famous men in history was writing an encouragement to a young man he knew, urging him to gallantly complete a difficult commission he had been given. In the course of it he reminded the young man of the splendor of the lives of his grandmother (Lois) and mother (Eunice), and in this way he urged him to live nobly.

The famous man was Paul, a special messenger of Jesus Christ, and his young friend was Timothy. And did the young man follow in the steps of his mother and grandmother, living his life nobly? Tradition says he became a leading figure for many years in the Christian movement in Ephesus and that he was clubbed to death by a ferocious mob because he publicly denounced the immorality of their worship of the Ephesian goddess, Artemis (Diana).

A grandmother and her daughter took a little boy of nervous temperament and helped shape him into a kind but bold spokesman for societal righteousness and decency. It shouldn't be hard for us to see Timothy giggling and thoughtful, wide-eyed and sleepy, quiet and questioning in the laps of the two most important and influential people in his life as he was being molded to play his part in the changing of the world for the better.

B. G. White's young woman was right: sometimes God takes something before it dies and makes it so beautiful—a white-haired, stooped little mother or grandmother, for example.

# A Far, Far Better Thing

✦

Whoever finds his life will lose it, and whoever
loses his life for my sake will find it.
—Matthew 10:39

I n Dickens's *Tale of Two Cities,* the prodigal young
lawyer, Sydney Carton, has fallen under the spell of
Lucie Manette, the doctor's daughter. He now realized he
has wasted his life and though he knows she can never
love him, he feels compelled to tell her how he feels about
her and how she has changed him. "I am like one who
died young," said Sydney. "All my life might have been."

She gently protests that better can be ahead for him,
but he insists it is too late. Assuring her that he will never

again in all his life so much as hint at what he is now say-ing, he pours out his sad soul in helpless gratitude to the one who has come to mean so much more to him than his own life. Finally, as he leaves, assuring Lucie that he isn't worth her tears, he says, "For you, and any dear to you, I would do anything. . . . When you see your own bright beauty springing up anew at your feet, think now and then that there is a man who would give his life to keep a life you love beside you."

Sometime later when Lucie's French aristocrat hus-band, Charles Darnay, is arrested in Paris and is to be exe-cuted by the revolutionaries, everyone is thrown into mad confusion except Sydney Carton. For the first time in his life his heart and mind agree on exactly what to do.

He makes the necessary arrangements and then spends the night walking through the streets reflecting on what he is about to do. Into his mind comes the Scripture that was read at his father's graveside: "I am the resurrection and the life, saith the Lord: he that believeth in me, though he were dead, yet shall he live: and whosoever liveth and believeth on me, shall never die."

The dying of the night and the coming of the sun seemed to drive home to him the truth he kept repeating as he wandered through the streets and down to the river.

And so, Carton, who looks remarkably like Lucie's husband, takes the place of Darnay and is executed in his stead.

Dickens tells us what Carton would have said just before dying had he been asked. Among other things, he would have said,

> I see the lives for which I lay down my life, peaceful, useful, prosperous and happy, in that

England which I shall see no more. I see her with a child on her bosom, who bears my name. I see a father, aged and bent, but otherwise restored, and faithful to all men in his healing office, and at peace. I see the good old man, so long their friend, in ten years time enriching them with all he has, and passing tranquilly to his reward.

I see that I hold a sanctuary in their hearts, and in the hearts of their descendants, generations hence. . . .

It is a far, far better thing that I do, than I have ever done; it is a far, far better rest that I go to than I have ever known.

And with that, the book ends.

What Carton did, did not begin with him. It began with Lucie Manette. She caught hold of his life by her loveliness and redeemed him.

It's a lovely thing to redeem those you care for, because there is such joy in the experience. Which of you, having made some wise, major sacrifices on behalf of those you love—which of you, seeing their usefulness and peace—regrets the price you had to pay? Doesn't your joy obliterate all regret? (Is this why a passage seems to speak of the Cross as the "joy set before" Jesus?)[1]

"He shall see the fruit of the travail of his soul and be satisfied," said the prophet of the Suffering Servant.[2] With God as his assurance, the Christ said of the time of his death, "I saw the Lord always before me, for he is at my right hand that I may not be shaken; therefore my heart was glad, and my tongue rejoiced."[3]

Carton saw the day when those he had given his life for would welcome the sound of his name. He saw their peace, usefulness and prosperity and knew that he would "hold a sanctuary in their hearts."

There will come a day when all the redeemers are in the presence of the Redeemer, and stories will be told. Sinners who were used by the Redeemer to bring other sinners to himself will tell their stories and there will be rejoicing everywhere.

It's a lovely thing to redeem those you love by dying for them. But maybe living for them until we die is dying for them too. There is more than one way to die for people.

# Selling and Smelling

✦

For we are to God the aroma of Christ
among those who are being saved
and those who are perishing.
—2 Corinthians 2:15

I was on my way to play squash with my friend and tough competitor, Len Moffat. He's the kind who won't stop playing until the match is over and we're back in the dressing room, so it was going to be another exhausting session.

To give me an edge I skipped lunch, but on the way up the hill to the club I passed a couple, sitting on a park bench eating fish and chips. Breakfast had been a long time ago and the smell nearly drove me crazy. Without a word, I stopped about two feet from them, licking my lips and devouring the aroma. They smiled at each other and said to me, "Want some?" With tremendous will power, I turned them down, but I went off with that lovely smell filling my thoughts. (It ruined my game. Len beat me like a drum. I should have eaten. Yes, that's it: I was too weak. I should have eaten.)

That couple didn't have to say a word about how tasty their lunch was—the fish and chips sold themselves. The aroma did it. The trouble with so many of us religious people is we spend more time "selling" than "smelling." (Even when we present the Bible to people, we're always stressing its "authority." We take one legitimate aspect of it and shut out all its winsomeness, adventure, and warmth.) There's a place for speech, sure, but even the speech has to have a winsomeness about it, if it's to do any good. I've argued enough in my day to know that intelligent discourse comes in a long way behind aromatic living.

> I've argued enough in my day to know that intelligent discourse comes in a long way behind aromatic living.

An ancient writer, Paul of Tarsus, spoke of Christians as "the aroma of Christ." That's a graphic phrase, isn't it? Christians are supposed to talk and walk, to sell and smell. Their speech and behavior are to blend together and make the offer of Christ appealing to discerning and needy people.

The story is told of a soldier who lay dying and the preacher who came to attend to him. "Can I help you in any way?" the young preacher asked. "I'm cold," snapped the dying man. "You don't have a blanket, do you?" In silence the minister took off his overcoat and spread it over him. The dying one glared at him a while. "My neck is hurting," he snarled in pain, and off came the minister's other coat to become a pillow. A few more moments of glaring and then a softer tone: "What about a cigarette?" The man lit him a cigarette and put it in his mouth—more moments of silence and a softening of heart despite the cold and the pain. Finally the soldier said to the conscientious, and obviously sad, young preacher, "Mister, if you've got anything in that Bible that makes you act like this, read it to me."

The preacher had a message to share, but sometimes words alone aren't welcome.

Believers don't have to be Jesus to get the world's attention. Most will forgive them their failings, but they must be honest failings, and there must be honest confession and contrition when appropriate. The most persuasive salesman in the world couldn't persuade anyone to buy aftershave or perfume that smells like sewage water.

Of course, Christians need to remember that they have a Story to tell and that it's the Story and the one who is the center of the Story who redeems, and not the aromatic living of his disciples. The lovely life of a Christian makes sense only within the context of that Story, so we're not permitted just to smell.

But believers must create a healthy hunger in those they influence. Children need to see lives worth imitating; they need to feel warmth that makes them feel assured and see faith that survives the storms of life. Nonbelievers should see glad-hearted justice modeled before them by believers; nonbelievers need to see the words and hymns and prayers of Christians matched by honest endeavor and to hear quick and genuine confession when the believer has been wrong. Only when they see what they feel the need of, only when they encounter what stirs the hidden hunger in them, will they be open to our speech.

THREE:

Redemption

♦

# Grounds for Believing

✦

Love never fails.

But where there are prophecies,

they will cease; where there are tongues,

they will be stilled; where there is knowledge,

it will pass away.

—1 Corinthians 13:8

In the midst of the sad, mad, bad world of his day, Jesus said to his followers, "Love one another with fervent and pure hearts,"[1] and "By this everyone will know you are my disciples, if you love one another."[2] And is there anything more redeeming than experiencing this? Even to watch it going on in the lives of others is redemptive.

Who needs to be convinced that there's evil in the world? Read the headlines or listen to the news on just about any day; look out the door on your own street; reflect a moment on your own family and life. The crime rates are spiraling, the prisons are overflowing, the nations are hacking each other to pieces, children are being abused before they're born as well as after, murderers become national heroes, art is steeped in filth, divorce is pandemic, cruelty is glamorized, and greed rapes the earth and its people.

"Love is . . ." all kinds of wonderful things; but in a world like ours, maybe the most astounding of all the things "Love is" is that it is at all! Wouldn't you think that in a world where the dog-eat-dog mentality is so prevalent there would be no self-sacrificing people? Wouldn't you think that with so many takers in the world there'd be no givers? Wouldn't you think that in a world where "Don't get mad, get even" comes to the lips of even children that there'd be no forgiveness? Aren't you tempted to think that in a world that glorifies immorality and marital treachery there'd be no men or women who cherish purity and lifelong fidelity? In a world of sleazy bars, porn centers, and drug barons, wouldn't you be inclined to think that sober, clean, socially useful people would have gone the way of the diplodocus? When you've seen (especially in the corridors of power) the piggy little eyes of savage greed running from one trough to another, stripping, devouring, hoarding, have you never been tempted to think that no one cares? No one? Not anywhere?

The amazing news is: Love is! Whatever the reasons, it seems that love just can't be killed. As long as God gives us mothers, fathers, brothers, and sisters, as long as God gives us families and friends, love will not only survive— it will flourish. Just as sure as a universe of darkness cannot snuff out a single candle ablaze with light, ten thousand universes saturated with hatred and heartlessness can't obliterate one loving act!

And the astonishing thing is, love doesn't beg to be given room; it doesn't grovel for permission to exist; it doesn't apologetically hang around the fringes of life as if it had no right to be there. Rather, it makes room for itself, comes right into the middle of life. Love is no weakling, no poor pathetic emotion that will vanish if someone breathes on it too hard. Even in the filthiest ghettos, the vilest homes, the most discouraging environments, it survives. You'll find it living among the garbage dumps of Mexico City and in the sewers of Colombia, in the teeming streets of Calcutta and in the sad hospitals of Zimbabwe. Love hangs out in universities, grade schools, and, yes, in Sunday schools too. Harder to believe but just as true, love is found alive in the Senate and Congress, in big business as well as in courtrooms. You'll even find love on the Falls or Shankill roads in Belfast; in Bagdad and Bosnia where mothers nurse their babies and sing their children to sleep.

Pain can drive people to madness. Prolonged suffering, injustice, and brutality can rob us of our sanity. Elie Wiesel, in his moving rehearsal of life under the Nazis, tells of sons who insanely killed their fathers to get all the bread rather than share what the fathers eagerly offered. No doubt incidents like these could be multiplied by thousands, but even there—where love was damned and in a billion different ways was hounded right out of the compounds—even there love, kept returning to life! Tormented with decisions no human should have to make, crying, cursing, almost despairing yet surviving, love remained stronger than torture and death, gentle as a lovely woman's heart.

And where did love like this come from? It certainly wasn't born in those camps! It was only tested there— deepened and made stronger there, purified and made wiser there. But that same love existed in the lives of all those millions long before Auschwitz or Treblinka came to be. Parents didn't *begin* to love their children in those hellholes. If those parents and children had not already loved one another, had not already been devoted to one another before they went to those damnable places, they never would have loved each other during their imprisonment and torture.

The love that went to Dachau was the same love that was nurtured through the years in spite of the world's selfishness. The love that was stuffed into cattle cars and then into ovens was the love that had for generations resisted the cynicism and sneering of the "good guys come last" philosophy. The kind of love that blazed so brightly in the death camps was the same love we see weeping in hospital waiting rooms or rocking in a chair, waiting, late into the night, for a teenage daughter to come home.

It's the same love we see in men and women who endure the torment of alcoholism in the family, who forgive marital infidelity and faithfully go on. And it's the same love we see in every man, woman, boy, and girl who lives sacrificially and joyfully, filling their world with goodness and kindness. When it found itself in Dachau or Siberia, it simply stepped up a gear. Lovers just held one another more tightly, watched out for one another more anxiously, longed after each other more tenderly, and defended each other more ferociously.

Critics of biblical theology have a lot of hard questions to ask believers, but I don't suppose they've ever asked any we haven't already asked ourselves. And most of us will admit that there are some questions we don't have fully satisfying answers for. Perhaps the most difficult question we're asked is: How do you explain the evil in the world if a good God is in control? I've learned some useful things to say in response to that question, but I admit that nothing fully satisfies me, so I say my piece and then point serious seekers in another direction.

But I wonder: how do unbelievers explain the presence of love in the world? I've read responses to this question, but they don't fully satisfy me. A world with evil in it raises questions about a good God, but a world with Jesus in it raises questions about no God. A world with Nazis in it raises serious questions for believers, but a world with sacrificial love raises serious questions for unbelievers.

As long as there is Jesus; as long as there are loving friends, parents, husbands, and wives; as long as there are those who do justice, love mercy, and walk humbly in the world, there are grounds for believing in God.

# Jessie Glencairn

✦

For none of us lives to himself alone and
none of us dies to himself alone.
—Romans 14:7

I n an old movie starring Jimmy Cagney, *Angels with
Dirty Faces,* Cagney plays the part of Rocky, a ruthless
criminal who is now making a big hit with the youth in
his old hometown. The kids follow Rocky's escapades
with smiles. They begin to act and talk like him, and they
begin to sneer at the work and words of a long-trusted
priest who was a boyhood friend of Rocky's.

The priest (played by Pat O'Brien) loves the gangster,
but hates that the boys see him as a hero and are model-
ing themselves after him. The priest pleads with Rocky to

put an end to it. The wisecracker laughs it off. Finally, he's arrested, tried, found guilty, and sentenced to die for killing some fellow-criminals. The teenagers are thrilled with Rocky's defiant attitude and even more set against goodness and uprightness.

The priest goes to the gangster on death row and pleads with him to kill his image in the eyes of the boys. His evil influence, his old friend tells him, will be even stronger after his death if he dies defiant and heroic. So for his friend's sake and for the sake of the kids, Rocky pretends to be a coward as he is taken to the electric chair. He begs and screams for mercy even while the guards are jeering at him for being "all sizzle and no steak."

Silly old movie. And yet . . . isn't it interesting how a lovely deed in an otherwise shabby life can take on a life of its own?

A thousand stories from fiction and daily living can illustrate the power of a lovely human life. Frank Boreham, in his book *The Three Half-Moons,* tells of an incident one evening when he and a group of friends were walking home. They passed an older man called Douglas, who had been nicknamed "Groggy" because he had been a hard drinker in his youth. That evening he looked as though he was shambling a bit, and one of the group thought he might have been drinking. Another who knew him better, however, said that was unlikely. Boreham, with some discreet and well-meaning inquiries, drew the conclusion that the old man had just come from the cemetery, which is where

> **Isn't it interesting how a lovely deed in an otherwise shabby life can take on a life of its own?**

Boreham headed. There on a corner was a grave adorned with fresh pink flowers. It was the grave and the birthday of Jessie Glencairn.

Boreham dropped by to see Douglas, found him in the garden and noted the clumps of pink carnations, but said nothing. A couple of years later, as if he were continuing a conversation, Groggy confessed that Jessie was the only woman he had ever loved. Said it was almost blasphemy for him to say he loved her because she was so far above him. He had been a terrible drunk, but from the day he looked straight into Jessie's eyes, he said, "I never troubled the drink again."

He knew it wasn't for the likes of him to love her, he said, but he would love to have seen Jessie marry a good man, even though it would have made him envious enough to have bitten his tongue off. Jessie never knew how Douglas felt about her, but one day, when they happened to be walking in the same direction, he told her that people were saying he would soon be back on the drink. "She gave me a look I'll never forget to my dying day," he said, "and told me she was certain I never would." Sometimes when the craving raged, he said, he seemed to see her with that look on her face and those words on her lips, and he felt he hated the stuff. However difficult it was, "I knew I'd be safe as long as I felt the same toward her."

"That," I fancied, "was the end of it," Borham said. "I forgot that a lovely life never ends."

When old Jamie McBride died thirty years later, one of his personal effects was a love letter written to him by Jessie Glencairn. She wrote of her grief that their sweet dreams of life together would have to be set aside because she had tuberculosis, which would soon kill her. While she couldn't allow Jamie to marry her, she told him, "I shall be proud, even on my deathbed, to think that you loved me and would have me as your wife. . . . I shall go down to my grave praying that the best things in this life may be always yours; and, if the dead can bless the living, I shall breathe constant benedictions on you and those who are dear to you."[1]

Boreham made this known to Groggy Douglas, who, when he thought about it for a while, went to the garden, gathered an armful of pink carnations, and divided them into two great bunches. These he laid on the lonely grave in the corner and on the fresh mound over Jamie McBride, who died unmarried.

"It is a luxury," said Boreham, "to be living in a world in which it is possible for a girl to die of tuberculosis in her thirties and yet to go on sweetening and brightening the lives of two lonely men, until blessing her memory, each of them, full of years and honor, goes down to his quiet grave."[2]

I forgot that lovely lives never end.

# "We'd Let Him in, Wouldn't We?"

✦

Here I am! I stand at the door and knock.

If anyone hears my voice and opens the door,

I will come in and eat with him, and he with me.

—Revelation 3:20

I t was July 11, 1971—a very good year. In Northern Ireland, that week of July means flute bands; processions of marchers thousands strong; Union Jack flags; curbstones painted red, white, and blue; streets decorated with mock city walls, streamers, and wall paintings; dancing in the streets; and bonfires at every other intersection. And there was booze—yes, plenty of booze—and pubs packed to the doors. This was the time when the

109

Protestant/Unionists celebrate an ancient victory over the Nationalist/Catholic forces.

One of the thousands of marchers in the "Orange Order" was Johnny Martin, who each year carried the symbolic saber as he marched triumphantly to the Field where the multitude, weary with the march, would be glad to sit and listen to a series of speakers calling them to maintain the Union (with Britain). Johnny was a painter by trade and a hard drinker by habit. I met Johnny when his wife, Peggy, was very ill with a cancer, which would brutally and swiftly rob her of life at the age of thirty-eight, forcing her to leave behind a daughter, Ethel, and two sons, Jackie and Roy. Later Johnny would remarry, and he and his devoted wife, Helen, would have a boy, Paul.

When Ethel and her daughter, Linda, went to see the bonfire one 11th of July, Johnny had already been drunk and sober several times that day. Up the street he came, well into another binge, extra whiskey in his pockets and plenty of time to get it down. He tried to cuddle his six-year-old granddaughter, Linda, but she began to cry big tears and to tell him she didn't like the way he smelled. That broke his heart, and then and there he swore to her that he would never drink again. That very night he gave his life to Christ, the booze was dumped, and Johnny Martin hasn't had a drop in over twenty years.

Marvelous! This kind of turnaround is by no means rare, but it's remarkable just the same.

It's funny how many things God uses in his attempts to turn us around. Even the things God doesn't actively bring our way (things like the birth of a baby suffering from spina bifida) can be used to touch our hearts. A tragic event, a lovely book, a splendid movie, the patience of a spouse, the suffering of innocent children, a close brush with death, the loyalty of a friend, the strength and gentleness of a physically big man. Six-year-old Linda's tears tugged on Johnny Martin's heartstrings.

A story is told of a man who took his little girl to an art gallery. She showed no interest at all until they came to a picture of a tired looking man, knocking and knocking on a door. The picture showed people on the other side of the door—it looked as if they had no plans to open it. She was hooked.

"Who is that?" she asked her dad. How could she know the question would trouble his heart—a heart that was wrestling with deep questions.

"It's Jesus," he heard himself say with a slight edge to his voice.

A pause, and then: "Won't they let him in?"

Unease began to grow in the man, but he could hardly brush her off, so he quietly said: "No they won't let him in."

Quick as light, she asked: "Is he bad?"

And he shot back just as fast: "No! He isn't bad."

Faster still, she demanded: "Well, then, why won't they let him in?"

Now he was really uneasy. He'd had enough, and as he gently but firmly walked her away from the picture, he heard himself say in a tone too terse: "How do I know?" She sensed the tension and said no more, but every now and then, big, dark, round eyes glanced at him and then in the direction of the portrait. She knew he knew something he wasn't telling her.

At supper no word was said about it, but the eyes kept talking. After supper she got ready for bed, and with pajamas on and with toothpaste still around her mouth, she climbed up on his lap and hugged his neck longer than usual. Then she kissed him, headed for the bedroom, stopped, turned, and said: "We'd let him in, wouldn't we?"

Then off she went to sleep like a rock, while all through a grown man's sleepless night God pried his heart open with a child's words.

I'm told that just like my father-in-law, Johnny Martin, the man "let him in."

◆

# Hastings Beauchamp Morley

✦

Where can I go from your Spirit?

Where can I flee from your presence?

—Psalm 139:7

Hastings Beauchamp Morley. How's that for a fine, upstanding name? Surely the man who wore that was without doubt an aristocrat of proven character.

In fact, he wasn't. He was a character in one of O'Henry's short stories, a character without character. The finest thing about him was his name after which came the way he dressed. ("Front, appearance does it. It's trumps in the game," he liked to tell himself.) He was a cheap crook and a swindler. With fake letters he would extract five

113

dollars from a missionary-minded clergyman, and with the same brilliance he would rob a little boy of eighty-five cents. His well-turned phrases and appearance bought him acceptance by the flighty upper crust, and his "sincere desire to help" enabled him to con a poorly dressed and anxious visitor to the big city out of all his cash.

But Hastings Beauchamp Morley was more than a swindler; he was a cynic. The world was filled with suckers and his vocation in life was to fleece them. And he was more than a swindling cynic, he was a self-righteous, swindling cynic. He would make things better for people, he told himself, if he were as rich as Rockefeller.

It filled him with satisfaction to throw a dollar to a nightly occupant of a park bench, cutting short the usual whining appeal. "God bless you!" said the grateful pauper. "I've been trying to find work for . . ." Morley called him a fool for thinking of work. "The world is a rock to you, no doubt; but you must be an Aaron and smite it with your rod. . . . That is what the world is for. It gives to me whatever I want from it."[1]

He walked on with a smile to the bright hotel where he'd get the best room and service with some of the fortune he'd stolen from a luckless stranger. What a great night it was, what a lovely moon, no one enjoyed a fine night better than he. Good luck followed him like a dog, he told himself, as he blew out plumes of smoke from his fine cigar. What a marvelous life! How could it get any better than this? What more could a man want?

The clock struck nine as a girl just entering womanhood stopped on the corner, waiting for a passing car. She was obviously hurrying home, maybe having worked late or some such thing. Her eyes were clear and pure and she was dressed in simple white.

Morley had known her at school. Eight years earlier he had sat on the same row. There had been no feelings between them—nothing but the friendship of innocent days. But as he looked, he suddenly knew he couldn't risk her seeing him. He turned down a side street to a quiet spot and laid his suddenly burning face against the cool iron of a lamppost. "God! I wish I could die," he said dully.

No matter how far we've wandered, no matter how far we think we've wandered, there's still that padding sound of the "hound of heaven" pursuing us. Hide behind what we will, cover ourselves with anything that comes to hand, and the God who made us and still loves us knows where we are. Just when we think we've finally shaken him off, that we've shut all the doors and windows against him; just when we're sure he has given up on us and that we can drift like debris, following the current to the dark depths of the abyss, a girl with pure eyes and a white dress rips to shreds the cheap facade and self-deceit we've thrown around us. There he is again.

A child with a trusting smile, a wife with a forgiving heart, a husband with strong tender ways, a grandmother quietly weeping, a "welcome home" when we expected to be shunned, a granddad who still adores and respects his wife fifty years down the road—with any one of these God nails us again. Just when we least expect it! *Please, leave me alone,* we beg in our worst, most weary moments. And then we're flooded with relief that bubbles up from some mysterious depth when we hear his quiet but decisive, *No!*

E. O. Wilson, materialist, atheist, and Darwinian, was the one, I'm told, who coined the word "sociobiology." He believes if we hate or love or are indifferent or whatever, it's because it's been programmed into our genes. In all kinds of ways Wilson has been saying to God, "Leave me alone." Robert Wright, in his book *Three Scientists and Their Gods,* tells what happened when the Pulitzer Prize-winning biologist attended a memorial service for Martin Luther King Jr. at Harvard.

In the middle of the service, which included a speech by King Sr. and many hymns, Wilson began to weep. Later, when asked why such a died-in-the-wool opponent of God wept, he explained that he hadn't been to such a service in so long and one of the hymns he remembered from years earlier had gotten to him. "It was the feeling that I had been a long way away from the tribe,"[2] he said. It was "merely tribal," he assured them.

Perhaps.

"Please, leave me alone."

"No."

# Maria and the Gangster

✦

And the parched ground shall become a pool,

and the thirsty land springs of water:

in the habitation of dragons, where each

lay [shall be] grass with reeds and rushes.

—Isaiah 35:7 KJV

We need people who come to stay! People who will stick it out even when it's tough and the road is long.

I won't waste time speculating long on how tough it must have been for so many Christian wives back in the days of the early church, but it couldn't have been easy. And I know this is a hard reality, but the apostle Peter spends no time in pouring out rivers of sympathy to these sweet and brave women. In 1 Peter 3, he moves, without fanfare, to the possible conversion of the unbeliever by the godly life of these beautiful women. The issue he stresses is the redemptive one—not how tough these wives might have it. Our temptation is to spend all our time sympathizing with the burdened believer, but the person who gets the consideration in this passage is the unbeliever. Compassion is a major virtue in our day (which is no bad thing), but wise compassion is needed even more. There is a time and place for us to remind one another that we are in the world as part of God's redemptive community. This redemptive work is to go on even at great personal cost. We learned that from our Master, didn't we?

Is it always easy to see our unbelieving spouse as one who is in terrible danger, as one who needs to be saved from him- or herself and the World Hater? Probably not. If the spouse is unkind and thankless, it is even more difficult. And if there are no signs whatever that he or she is beginning to look in God's direction even after some years, well, that can be a recipe for collapse. Under tough circumstances, sympathy is certainly called for, but in a society where "throwing in the towel" when things are difficult is on the increase, sympathy can be a weakening thing if it isn't dispensed wisely.

**In a society where "throwing in the towel" when things are difficult is on the increase, sympathy can be a weakening thing if it isn't dispensed wisely.**

Michael Green, a much published English churchman, in a story called "Jesus Spells Freedom," tells of seventeen-year-old Maria Sorensino. In the 1940s Ezio Barberi and his ruthless gang achieved fame in Italy as a result of brutal murders and armed robberies. In 1949 Barberi was sentenced to fifty-seven years in the maximum security wing of San Vitorre prison in Milan. He was a thug outside, and he was a thug inside. He was involved in violence and rioting in the jail, and as is often the case, he had his cell walls covered with pornography.

What has all this to do with Maria? Well, for some reason, Maria had fixed her eye on Barberi and kept a scrapbook of the gangster's moves and escapades. She took him into her heart and prayed for him every day. They had never met, but she began to write to him in prison. She pleaded with him for change, expressed her love for him, and despite his violent and ugly spirit, she made a commitment to him and wouldn't turn from it.

Gradually, Barberi began to change. Being on the receiving end of a love like that, said Green, began to transform him. He began to write to Maria, and he ripped the porn off his wall and put her picture up. He responded to her tender letters with tenderness such as he had never shown to anyone. His violent behavior ceased, and he became a model prisoner. He involved himself in the work of the hospital, charity endeavors, and socially useful works.

What happened to the cold-blooded, hate-filled criminal? *Someone had come to stay.* Someone paid the price for years without complaint, and on June 18, 1968, twenty-one years (believe I'll say that again: *twenty-one years*) after Maria had entered Ezio's life, they were married in the prison chapel.

Yes, I know about the common "failures" of loving commitment (though nothing lovingly and honorably given is ever wasted), but people like Maria Sorensino are a sight for sore eyes in a world where cruelty, ingratitude, and self-service get center stage. They are a rebuke to all this bleating and whining about how hard it is to hang in when things are tough or not moving as quickly in the right direction as we would wish. (I have no criticism, whatever, for those who for years have endured pain so stark that to be glib about it would be obscene. I have no criticism for those who, having endured this state of affairs, decided to call the relationship to a halt. How could I, whose life has been so easy, throw stones?)

I'm wondering as I write this if there is anyone, alive or dead, who could say of us that we came to stay, and stayed? I'm wondering if there is anyone, alive or dead, that we pursued for Christ's sake even though it cost us much in endurance. I'm wondering if there is anyone for whom we have dismissed the trouble as simply part of the price we (and many others like us) have to pay to be God's agent of redemption.

Ringing in my ears and coming from a cattle shed, a garden, and a cross are the patient words and wounds of one who said: "I will never leave you nor forsake you."[1]

FOUR

# HOPE

The Christian hope is not
simply a trembling, hesitant
hope that perhaps the
promises of God may be
true. It is the expectation
that they cannot be
anything else than true.
			—William Barclay

✦

# The Hope-Bringing Story

✦

> Though you have not seen him, you love
> him; and even though you do not see him
> now, you believe in him and are filled
> with an inexpressible and glorious joy.
>
> —1 Peter 1:8

King Arthur conceived the idea of a round table at which all the nobles' knights could sit in unity and plot the downfall of the land's great wrongs. Just when the face of England was changing, when men no longer had to lock their doors and women could walk unafraid where they wished, Guinevere and Lancelot came together in dishonor. After an initial bend toward revenge, the king wanted to forgive, but the knights talked of treason and Guinevere was tried, found guilty, and sentenced to be killed. Lancelot came to her rescue and carried her off to France. The die was cast: there would be war between Lancelot's forces and the Knights of the Round Table.

On the morning of the battle, when the terribly depressed Arthur was donning his armor, he heard a noise in the bush. When called, a boy, Tom of Warwick, came out saying he was ready to do battle against the king's enemies and die if necessary. He wanted to be a knight, he said.

A knight? Why would he want to be a member of that extinct profession, the king asked him. Was his father a knight? No. Was his mother ever rescued by a knight? No. What then did he know of knights? Only the stories he had been told.

**Maybe today we're more bored than we realize; maybe we've set our eyes on things that blunt the edge of our hunger for the highest.**

The despairing king was suddenly seized by the grandeur of the thought, and hope arose again in his heart. Maybe all was not lost. "What stories?" he wanted to know. And as the boy talked of round tables, might for right and justice for all, the king was mouthing the words along with him. The ideal was still alive! It hadn't died despite the failure of individuals. The power of the stories continued to keep it alive in the hearts of those who had the ears to hear.

The New Testament writer of Hebrews told his readers that where they now were was better than where they had been, what they now had was better than what they once had, and who they now followed was greater than whom they had once followed. It was true, he insisted, that these disciples had not yet seen all they had hoped for, but it was also true, he said, that "we see Jesus."[1] For him, that was *vision enough.*

The apostle Peter wrote to people who were always looking at or for things they did not currently see. They lived their lives despite the thunder of appearances. In the Bible, this isn't nonsense or whistling in the dark; it isn't a lack of realism. It's vision and faith. These people trusted themselves in love to a Savior they hadn't seen. They were pilgrims—not only in some religious sense—they were quite literally (socially and politically) non-citizens, and some were even homeless (passing through). In their vulnerability, belonging to the family of God brought joy to their souls. To be wanted by the Lord, even a lord they hadn't met and couldn't see, gave them the joy of their lives, joy so wondrous they couldn't express it.

"Though you have not seen him, you love him; and even though you do not see him now, you believe in him and are filled with an inexpressible and glorious joy."[2] Their joy was in response to their vision, and their vision was what their eye of faith saw.

But *inexpressible and glorious joy?* That kind of joy on the strength of a mere vision, a commitment of faith? Maybe today we're more bored than we realize; maybe we've set our eyes on things that blunt the edge of our hunger for the highest; maybe this Savior of ours is less to us because other things are more. Maybe we don't feel the sense of "not belonging" here that the pilgrims Peter addressed felt. Perhaps if we felt our homelessness more,

we'd be more joy-filled at the thought of him and his coming.

And where did these Christians get their vision? They hadn't met the Master; they weren't able to see him so they didn't get it in his physical presence. They got it from the *Story*.[3] They were told the biblical Story, an old Story, a truth-filled Story, about a God who came in search of a lost world.

Those who think stories are weak aren't thinking straight. People are shaped and live by the stories they tell and have been told. You only have to reflect on how powerful lies are, the effects of a piece of slander, to know that there is power in stories. (Think of Jacob's response to the story that Joseph had been killed.)[4]

Stories are most powerful when they're the truth, because no lie lives forever. In an infinitely more profound way, the truth of Jesus Christ is kept before the hearts and minds of the world by the Story—the true Story that creates vision and has the substance Arthurian legend lacks. And while lies and fiction, even lovely fiction, pass away, those who have found truth and vision in Jesus Christ have been born of a Word that abides because it remains the truth forever.[5]

This vision not only has power to see the future, it is part of that future, already in existence. It not only looks for the new heavens and earth in which righteousness dwells, it is part of it already.

# To See Jesus Is to Hope

✦

Be joyful in hope, patient in affliction,

faithful in prayer.

—Romans 12:12

U nchanging appearances can kill hope. The same
enemies year after year. The same difficulties time
after time. Failed methods, failed plans, failed attempts
can kill hope. "I keep trying. I'm tired of trying. Nothing
changes, nothing makes any difference. The brutal fact is
that nothing can be done about the way things are. I'm
weary of pep talks and pop psychology. It all sounds great
until I turn to face reality."

Is that hard to understand? I've felt (and at times still
feel) like that. It's not difficult to understand. Still, if

things are so bad, why do we still feel in our bones that they will get better? How do we explain that renewed sense of hope even after months or years when everything seems to be such a dead heave?

We continue to hope because we've "seen" something. Someone!

Though we have not seen our Lord and Savior with our eyes, like the brave men and women to whom Peter wrote, we continue to hope for our salvation. Peter spoke of a salvation not yet revealed,[1] a goal for which they aimed,[2] a hoped-for inheritance.[3] In Peter's second letter he describes these hopeful people as looking for a new heaven and a new earth. And they looked forward to this new world simply on the basis of his promise.[4]

What so seized them that they held on so strongly to what they could not see? It was their vision of the Christ who was to be revealed,[5] the Christ they had come to love because of the Story they had heard about him and by which they had been born into a new life.[6] It was because they had a vision of him that they were willing to be his pilgrims, joyfully on the move in this world as they waited for another. It was because their trust in him and love of him was so strong that they were glad to experience something of salvation while they waited for the completion of that salvation.[7]

It's true they were still traveling toward something they hadn't actually, or at least fully, seen, but they had seen enough to know their journey was well spent. We, along with the readers who maintained their trust despite appearances, can say:

— We don't see all the crooks behind bars, but we see Jesus.

– We don't see the porn industry permanently shut down, but we see Jesus.

– We don't see the drug bosses out of business forever, but we see Jesus.

– We don't see the vice rings smashed for all time, but we see Jesus.

– We don't see the ugliness of our own lives banished, but we see Jesus.

– We don't see the street gangs dismantled or crooked cops removed, but we see Jesus.

– We don't see the growth within us that we've longed for, but we see Jesus.

– We don't see any reason to believe the world is getting any better, but we see Jesus.

– We see the uncleanness in our own hearts, but we see Jesus.

– We see our trivial ways and pathetic goals, but we see Jesus.

– We see broken promises, shattered families, and the defeat of noble programs, but we see Jesus.

– We see the increasing number of the vulnerable aged and the depletion of resources and massive unemployment, but we see Jesus.

– We see pain, agony, wickedness. We see all of that. But we see Jesus.

They looked the world right in the eye, saw it for what it was, and with confident smiles got on with living. In doing this they were like their father in the faith, Abraham, of whom the Hebrew writer said: "By faith Abraham, when he was called to go to a place he would later receive as his possession, obeyed and went, even though he did not know where he was going. By faith he made his home in the promised land like a stranger in a foreign country; he lived in tents . . . For he was looking forward to the city with foundations, whose architect and builder is God."[8]

Is this not nonsense? Can people really live that way? Of course they can! They do it in every city in every generation!

It's my suspicion that the vast majority of us have never become desperate enough to know the utter joy of complete dependence on Jesus Christ. When we have no other props—like "sufficient" money in the bank, paid-up insurance, a steady job, better than good health, a devoted family, and loads of friends—we then discover just how assuring Christ can be. My guess is that we rely on these other fine blessings from God, and thus they work us harm. Wasn't it the Christ who said that the eye or the hand or the foot might sometime offend us?[9] These fine blessings from God might have to be put from us before we really enter into life—not just hereafter, but now! With the lovely props all gone or nearly gone, we will be thrown back onto the Christ as our soli-

> **It's my suspicion that the vast majority of us have never become desperate enough to know the utter joy of complete dependence on Jesus Christ.**

tary means of support. Maybe then we'll find, as count-less thousands through the years have found, that Christ is altogether grand and comes to mean more to us than before. With the props gone, we have the opportunity to rejoice with joy inexpressible and glorious.

# The Prisoner of Chillon

✦

We live by faith, not by sight.

—2 Corinthians 5:7

I t is vision that creates and sustains our hopes, and it
is vision that won't allow us to settle for less than we
can attain.

When we meet the Christ, the living Christ, we come
to life again. With faith that springs from the depth of
our joy, we run to the trash cans to retrieve the dreams
and hopes we'd thrown away in our despair. Eagerly we
pull them out, dust them off, and find to our joyful
amazement that they are not only still intact, they are glo-

riously enhanced. They are richer, stronger, and more beautiful than they had been. And we turn to Christ with a new light in our eyes, showing him our dreams in speechless thankfulness. "I know," he says, "they were fine before, but I did something to them. They're even better now."

And then we turn to an onlooking world, a world with empty eyes despite its seeing so much, a world with a hungry soul despite its gorging so much. A world that, for all its talk of guiding its own destiny and creating its own future, has become cynical and has learned to love despair. And we say, "See? We have hope and dreams again! Life isn't a weary plod toward the dark or a mindless march to oblivion. There are worlds ahead, glorious and deathless, where corruption and defilement have no place. There's an inheritance ahead for all who still care or wish they could still care. We have met Someone who opened our eyes by opening our hearts. He has faced the worst nightmares we ever knew, the deepest darkness we ever wandered through, the most crushing defeats we've ever suffered, and the abysmal sense of abandonment we've suffocated under. He triumphed over all these and has brought us the message that God wishes us no harm!

> **We have met Someone who opened our eyes by opening our hearts.**

People need this message of hope! Listen carefully and you'll hear the sigh of a world that has everything to live with and nothing to live for. Boredom and satiation are killing our lands more surely than acid rain or ecological disasters. We're visionless and so, pulling our shroud more tightly around ourselves to keep out the chilling and deepening cold, we wait for the coming of the last great sigh before eternal silence reigns.

Even the atheist Bertrand Russell felt the poignancy of it all. Speaking of apes in the zoo, when they were not cracking nuts or doing their gymnastic routines, he said there seemed to be in their eyes a strange, strained sadness—as if they knew their human cousins had left them behind while they themselves had gone down a dead end of evolution. They seemed to know there was something better, but they didn't know how to get it.

Then with added sadness, Russell said it seemed to him that that same strange, strained sadness was in the eyes of civilized man. Looking at himself, he felt in his bones that there was something better if only he could find his way to it.

An endless history of failure can lead to a sense of helpless despair, and the light of hope can go out. We can become content with nothing! Lord Byron's poem, "The Prisoner of Chillon,"[1] is more poetry than history about the experiences of a gentleman called Bonaventure, who spent some time in prison. For years the prisoner suffers the loneliness of isolation, which wounds and crushes and narrows his spirit until he becomes accustomed to it. By and by he makes friends of spiders and little earth beetles; and beaten down by the sameness of the passing years, he becomes a prisoner not only in body but in mind as well. To be read in a dull, flat tone, Byron has him tell us,

> It was at length the same to me,
> fettered or fetterless to be.
> I learned to love despair.

But what if, as Gossip imagined, after years of silence, gloom, contentment with lower things, and love of despair—what if the prisoner spies the window high in the cell wall and on a whim decides to climb to it and look out. Fighting through many failures, his fingers finally reach the ledge. With only enough strength to pull himself up for a few seconds, he sees outside his prison window a blue sky, white clouds, cavorting birds, and not far away, across a stretch of clear blue water, a green land with a neat row of whitewashed cottages on a little hill. Imagine him, then, as he half falls, half slides back down into the gloom. Will the prison not now be a coffin? Won't the darkness and gloom now suffocate him and will he not now beat on the door of his prison shouting, "I've got to get out; I've got to get out! Dear God, I must get out of here!"?

And do we think this is only a poem, only imagination? Haven't we seen this, you and I, again and again? People who live alone in the twilight, crippled by criticism and crushed by injustice. Timid and afraid, always fretting and instinctively covering their heads and hearts against expected blows. Then to their astonishment, they come across someone who loves them, who really does love them, and heaps on them judicious praise and calls them to richer living. Something like a miracle happens; they begin to unfold like a flower in the sun and change into the most amazing and glorious people.

I've seen it—and so have you—in the eyes of people who worried long years under the fear that God will in the end cast them aside, too weak to be saved, not productive enough. Under that fear they lack enthusiasm, they have no story to tell of what the Lord has done for them. Then they hear a Story of grace that covers all their sin and enlists them in an incredible adventure. Their eyes light up, their face breaks into a smile, joyful amazement springs to life, and they are changed forever.

The message for us all is that it's all right to hope again! Light has broken through the darkness. We are free—free to dream and to rejoice in the glory of those dreams because God has broken down the prison walls we built for ourselves and has set us free.

A whole new world of hope has come into being.

♦

# "I Am Lazarus"

✦

Whether he is a sinner or not, I don't know. One
thing I do know. I was blind but now I see!
—John 9:25

Hope is not mere wishing or longing—it is expecting, a confident expecting. When hope is present,
there is that sense of assurance that things are going to be
better, that they're going to come to a satisfying conclusion.

Personal failure and difficult living conditions will cast
their vote against hope, especially if they're around a long
time and have powerful allies to give them help. What
sustains hope must have enough power to take all that on
and overcome it.

Our hope is alive and well because it comes "through the resurrection of Jesus Christ from the dead."[1] We sometimes face difficulties but none more difficult than what our Master faced. The voices raised against our hope are no stronger than those that mocked the Christ as he hung on the cross ("He trusted in God, let's see if God will deliver him"). The powers that stand shoulder to shoulder against us are no more entrenched or powerful than those that plotted and executed their cruelty against Jesus.

So Christ's victory is our assurance, our ground for hope: "In this world you will have trouble. But take heart! I have overcome the world."[2] To know he has done it lifts the heart. To know he has done it for *us* lifts the heart even further. We're pleased for all the struggling souls that finally see the light of day and scramble from the darkness in which they've been imprisoned. Their victory gives us some reason to hope that we, too, will experience triumph over the powers that assault and wound us. But when we realize that Christ's victory was won for *us*, we have reason to rest assured that the longing we feel is well grounded. We will win because in Jesus Christ we have won. Yes, appearance will continue to have its say and sometimes we'll experience an emotional downer, but Christ is alive! He is alive and has been raised not only for himself but for us.[3]

If Christ really has risen to glorious life after death, that single fact is enough to offset all the plausible stories

> **Our hope is alive and well because it comes "through the resurrection of Jesus Christ from the dead."**

that are spun by the cynics, pessimists, and enemies. If Christ is truly risen, the rest doesn't matter.

G. K. Chesterton made that point vivid to us in his poem called "The Convert." It articulates the response of Lazarus, who has just been brought out of the tomb by Jesus Christ:

> After one moment when I bowed my head
> And the whole world turned over and came
>     upright,
> And I came out where the old road shone white,
> I walked the ways and heard what all men
>     said. . . .
> The sages have a hundred maps to give
> That trace their crawling cosmos like a tree,
> They rattle reason out through many a sieve
> That stores the sand and lets the gold go free:
> And all those things are less than dust to me
> Because I am Lazarus and I live.[4]

Picture him walking down the road, stopping to listen to a group of wise old heads debating the possibility of life after death and proving beyond doubt, with unanswerable arguments, that the hope of it is a fool's dream. See Lazarus smile to himself and leave them to their profound conclusions. "I am Lazarus, and I'm alive!"

And don't you remember the man who had been born blind but Jesus said, "Let there be light!" and there was? Remember how they kept asking the man questions he couldn't answer? They baffled him with theology, baffled him with medical questions, baffled him with the "impossible" nature of it all. We can see him shaking his head as he admitted he couldn't answer their questions. But one fact, one solid, inescapable truth was known to him: "Once I was blind, but now I see!" The theological questions, the arguments that might "prove" it couldn't have been done (especially by a "sinner" like Jesus)—all that needed answering no doubt. But whatever the answers, the fact remained: he had been blind and now he could see! That one truth, like Jesus' resurrection, was the test of everything else!

As a universe of darkness can't put out the light of a single candle, so all the arguments, difficult questions, and passionate denials cannot obliterate a single fact: Jesus is alive! And if he lives, righteousness wins! Honor wins! Holy dreams come true! Longing hearts are comforted and holy hunger is satisfied. Friendships in God last forever, sorrow is banished, and cruel death is put to death. If he lives, all of this is not just idle talk, not just whistling in the dark, not just empty words! If he's alive, Sin, Sorrow, and Death have been served notice. This One who "got away" is the beginning of an innumerable host who will dance on the graves of Sin and Death forever!

# "We Had Hoped"

✦

How foolish you are, and how slow of heart to
believe all that the prophets have spoken!
—Luke 24:25

Appearances can kill hope; but appearances are
shaped by the story we buy into. If we believe the
wrong major story, we will see life in light of that flawed
master story. If we believe a story that takes only some of
the facts into account, we will see life in a distorted way.

On the road to Emmaus, you remember, two men met
a stranger who wanted to know what they were discussing
that had them looking so sad.[1] They told him of things
that had happened in Jerusalem. "What things?" he
wanted to know. "About Jesus of Nazareth," they told

him. "He was a prophet, powerful in word and deed before God and all the people. The chief priests and our rulers handed him over to be sentenced to death, and they crucified him; but we had hoped that he was the one who was going to redeem Israel."

"We had hoped . . ." Their glum faces, their sad hearts, the stubborn facts—these all witnessed to the truth that "had hoped" was the right phrase. Harsh realities have a way of killing hope. Harsh realities have a way of killing hope even if it is grounded in the right person. Deep disappointment preaches powerfully; it's very persuasive. Bone-deep pain isn't easily overcome, even when wise words of truth are spoken. The sight of a screaming, leukemic child shuts out just about everything else, even a word from God. The horrific sight and sounds of Auschwitz killed the faith and hope in the heart of the teenage child, Elie Wiesel, who with millions of others said, "We had hoped." For all kinds of reasons and in all sets of circumstances, people have dropped down listless with disappointment, dry-eyed with weeping, and flat with despair.

John Vannorsdall, in a riveting piece, has expressed for us this deep sense of disillusionment at broken visions and long-delayed or crushed hopes. Beginning with the two on the road he allows us all to become part of the experience:

> There was a time when we thought that the world could be a better place. We were capable of visions, you see. We could imagine a world of green lawns rather than a street full of junk, a world where neighbors greeted one another rather than pass silent with hidden faces, a world in which the aged were wise and cherished,

where bullies were defeated, where games were for fun rather than profit, and dancing was the purest pleasure.

We had a vision of a world of clean, white snow, smelling of spring, carpeted with autumn's color. There was a time when we thought the world could be a better place.

There was a time when we thought that we could be better persons.

We could imagine our families proud of us rather than ashamed. Imagine a crucial time when we would dare to tell the truth and everyone would be amazed and say, "Thank God the truth's been told at last." We could imagine a time when we would be the champion for some kid beaten on the street, or be the lawyer fighting for the innocent and oppressed. We would be the scientist discovering a way to feed the hungry, an engineer making heavy work light. There was a time when we thought we could be better persons.

◆

There was a time when we believed that God had a plan for his people. His plan was to bless marriage with joy and children, to free us of our sins and guilt, fill our lives with peace, to remake the world without war, a world in which the woods were cool on a summer's day and the animals played with one another. There was a time when we believed that God had a plan for his people.

"We had hoped," said the two on the road to Emmaus, "that he was the one to redeem Israel."2

Doesn't that piece just beg to be heard? Doesn't he put his finger on just the right spot, touching us where it hurts, leading us to say with genuine sadness, "Yes, just there, that's the place; that's where it hurts"?

But it's right there, where it hurts, the place where our hopes fell down, stone dead at our weary, wandering feet—there, the living, resurrected Jesus confronts us with the sure word that we've only been hearing part of the story.

That is both the glory and the scandal of our faith, that the living Lord wants to set his one living, vibrant truth over against all the other harsh realities and truths. It is scandalous of him to ask us to trust and hope—yes, hope!—and continue to hope, in the face of all these bruising realities. And it is the glory of our faith that it has been powerful enough to enable people to be born again, to live again, to be resurrected in hope. Not a grim, teeth-clenched existence, but joy-filled life in the midst of tribulation.

And as the word he spoke to the pair on the road to Emmaus reaches our own hearts, it isn't surprising that their experience becomes ours, and we find ourselves enjoying the warmth of life coursing through our hearts. "Holy heartburn."

No wonder Peter says, in that sentence in which every word is an education: "Praise be to the God and Father of our Lord Jesus Christ! In his great mercy he has given us new birth into a living hope through the resurrection of Jesus Christ from the dead."[3]

# The God of Good Hope

✦

May the God of hope fill you with all joy and
peace as you trust in him, so that you may over-
flow with hope by the power of the Holy Spirit.

—Romans 15:13

William Manson, so we're told, had one sentence
constantly on his lips: "The only God the New
Testament knows is the God of resurrection."

That makes sense, and it's that truth—that the God of
the Scriptures is a God who gives life to the dead—that
undergirds any hope we have of life now or hereafter. It's
that truth that strikes Giant Despair dead at our feet and
calls us to look Death right in the eye—Death in all its
forms and appearances, Death now and Death later—and

spell out its doom. "A living hope," said Peter, comes to us from God "through the resurrection of Jesus Christ from the dead."[1]

Hebrews 13:20–21 rings out this message:

> May the God of peace, who through the blood of the eternal covenant brought back from the dead our Lord Jesus, that great Shepherd of the sheep, equip you with everything good for doing his will, and may he work in us what is pleasing to him, through Jesus Christ, to whom be glory for ever and ever. Amen.

What a picture of Christians is given here—fully equipped with everything good to do God's will and so shaped as to be pleasing to him. And how is this accomplished? Through Jesus Christ! The Jesus Christ whom God brought back from the dead, the resurrected Jesus Christ, the having-defeated-death Jesus Christ.

As J. S. Stewart reminded us, our litany of failures, our present weakness, our broken promises, our half-decency—all these would urge us to keep our dreams within bounds, to be modest in our expectations because of the harsh realities we know about ourselves and the world we have to live in.

This all sounds reasonable and sensible. The humility may even be commendable, says Stewart, "But before we accept it as final or inevitable, let us have another look at what the apostle is saying. . . . He begins with God . . . with God in one particular aspect. He begins with the God of the resurrection." Yes! "Before we start arguing what is possible or not possible in the Christian life, let us get our standpoint right."[2]

Does the psychologist or social worker know that we fear tomorrow because of the specters of unemployment, old age, disease, loneliness, a sense of uselessness, or death?

Does God know less?

And what is the cure for such fears?

Will the psychologist or social worker guarantee that the worrier won't grow old? Can the worrier be promised he won't become unemployed, diseased, or lonely, that he won't feel useless or die?

Who can guarantee that? How is the worrier to be relieved? Will we tell him that the things he worries about aren't as bad as they seem? But they are as bad as they seem! To worry about these things is not to worry about trivia; to humans they're of great importance. To speak of them as if they didn't matter is only to make matters worse and to lose credibility.

So if we can't guarantee exemption from them, what's our alternative? We might sit sympathizing and wringing our hands along with the sufferer, but if that's all there is, we're all in trouble. We cry out for more than hand-wringers and people to sympathize with us.

What is it the Christian has to say that can make a difference? Does he deny that the future holds these things? No, he just adds *God* to old age, unemployment, disease, loneliness, uselessness, and death. Ahead of us is God! And if the God who is up ahead of us is like Jesus Christ, then we can face all these things with hope burning in our hearts.

God smites death with resurrection. He gives purpose to those who feel useless and whispers the assurance of his presence to the lonely. He brings loved ones together who have been separated in death. There is no death he cannot heal, no separation he cannot obliterate, no loss he cannot deal with. Find that in the philosophy books, the psychologist's office, the Mayo clinics, or the insurance policies!

The psalms are crammed with people who find themselves up to their necks in trouble but who are sure that God has not forsaken them. Or, if for a while he "turns his face" from them (brings or permits trouble), they're sure that things will turn out right again. So bravely they face the hardships and insist on turning to no one but the Lord, who is ever watching them and has shown his devotion to them through the years.

It is to a young church that is having trouble with its neighbors that Paul gives the challenge to remain loyal to the Story he had brought to them. "May our Lord Jesus Christ himself and God our Father, who loved us and by his grace gave us eternal encouragement and good hope, encourage your hearts and strengthen you in every good deed and word."[3]

"Eternal encouragement and good hope!" This comes, not because we're well thought of, not because our health is fine, our financial future is secure, our friends are packed tightly around us, and our neighborhood is free from violence. It comes because God loves us and has been gracious to us. This, and nothing less, is what has made us alive again unto a living hope!

Forgi

rgiveness

# FIVE

# FORGIVENESS

I said a foolish thing; I
wish I could unsay it. But
you alone can unsay it
by not remembering my
foolishness when you
remember me.

                    —Charles Morgan

                    ◆

# Forgiveness Is Not Cheap

✦

Be kind and compassionate to one another,

forgiving each other, just as in Christ

God forgave you.

—Ephesians 4:32

To say something very profound about the rich notion of forgiveness is not only beyond the scope of this little book, it is beyond my competence. But it won't hurt to say some things in passing.

It's only in speech or writing that forgiveness is thought to be easy or cheap. When it comes to practicing it, we can find a hundred reasons (good reasons, of course!) why we shouldn't forgive. Far removed from actual offenses, painful and often-repeated offenses, we can talk glibly about forgiving. But when we have been gouged—or worse, when some much-loved friend or family member has been gouged—when that happens, the words about forgiveness are sometimes dismissed or qualified beyond recognition. This may be perfectly understandable but it underscores the reality we wrestle with in this area.

Still, we mustn't expect badly wounded people to dispense forgiveness the way a vending machine dispenses candy bars. There aren't many things harder to watch than a serious offender further hurt the one he's wounded by virtually demanding forgiveness even while the wounded one is anguished with the pain. We can't demand what can only be a gift of grace!

As World War II ended, numerous guards and camp commandants sought forgiveness from those they treated so horrendously and were refused it. Is that really surprising? I'm not saying forgiveness should have been withheld; I just want to make the point that a lot of glib rot is spoken about forgiveness by those who've never suffered deeply at the hands of transgressors.

> A lot of glib rot is spoken about forgiveness by those who've never suffered deeply at the hands of transgressors.

So I'm saying that forgiveness doesn't come easy to people who've been terribly used and abused. Even the saintly Corrie ten Boom confessed at one point to having a very difficult time indeed forgiving her Nazi enemies. When we see remarkable cases of forgiveness in the face of awful sin we're amazed and inspired by it. If it were common to see horrific transgressions graciously forgiven, we'd cease to be amazed.

My limited observation of life suggests it's often the very upright and law-abiding people (or those who see themselves in this light) who have an especially tough time forgiving. They often lack patience and tolerance with offenders. The fact that their own lives are under control, that their behavior and speech are impeccable, leads them to believe that everyone's life should be like that. If they can control themselves, they reason, it must be that everyone can—if indeed they wish to. If they aren't controlled, why then they must not wish to be controlled; and if they don't wish to be controlled, they should not be forgiven.

I've seen this in people from whom you'd least expect it. It's not uncommon in recovered alcoholics who, having struggled for years, have finally beaten this awful addiction and returned to normal life. Since they have beaten it, they seem to reason that anyone can—if he or she really wants to. Self-righteousness creeps in and impatience increases toward those who don't seem to be "trying hard enough." It's all very understandable. I think this explains, in part, why it was that Jesus always seemed to be in trouble with the righteous and law-abiding people of his time. These people really were decent and upright. They weren't sinless, of course, but they weren't degenerates either. And because their behavior was so different from the majority of those around them, they became too hard—and it's a sin to be too hard!

The Bible, and the New Testament in particular, makes it very clear that forgiveness is not "easy" for God, since he experiences a holy recoil from evil. Whatever else the Cross of Christ may teach us, the Christian would say, it teaches us that forgiveness is no cheap and easy transaction.

I'm not saying that God had to be persuaded by the atoning death of Jesus Christ to forgive us. That would be missing the fact that the death of Christ was God's gift to us and that his death was the means by which God worked our forgiveness. But however the death of Christ is related to the forgiveness of sin—whatever his death's precise connection with our forgiveness is—the New Testament teaches us that his death was essential to our forgiveness. And that being true, forgiveness can hardly be seen as cheap or common.

Forgiveness is a complex reality. Those who dismiss injustice and oppression as of no consequence know nothing of forgiveness. To believe there is really nothing to answer for means that forgiveness is redundant. But those who believe that forgiveness is and must be a reality necessarily bring in things like: admitting guilt (sin exists, and I did wrong); accepting responsibility (I can't place the blame on others); renouncing the sin (I recognize the evil of what I've done and denounce it); purposing to avoid it in the future (I know I may face the temptation again, and I determine now to avoid it); and trusting the grace of the wounded or dishonored ones (I can't demand that they put the offense aside and go on as before).

We must resist the temptation to place all offenses on the same level and to demand that others place all offenses on the same level. Those who can't forgive an occasional act of rudeness without making a major production out of it have a problem of their own to deal with. Those who believe that it's as simple to forgive the torture, rape, and murder of a child as it is to forgive a stream of foul language yelled by an angry person need to think this whole matter through again. (This is not to deny that all sins are in need of forgiveness. They are!)

Because there are so many variables in the lives of people, we need to recognize that the creative and gracious act of forgiveness takes on different features in different settings. To equate forgiveness with a brisk "It's okay; it's no big deal!" or "It's all right; it doesn't matter!" misses the point. Forgiveness, if it's real, doesn't support the notion that nothing wrong has happened. But a forgiving heart doesn't act as though every unkind act or remark must be dragged out into the open before it is forgiven either. Different situations will mean that forgiveness is worked in different ways. To say to a Nazi commandant: "It's okay; it's no big deal!" not only insults all the dishonored and wounded victims, it violates the sinner and brings self-condemnation on ourselves who should know better.

The Bible plainly teaches that forgiveness and chastisement aren't enemies—they can go hand in hand. It's clearly possible for a person or a group of people to forgive a man for embezzling their money on several occasions, but it may be to the benefit of all concerned (the offender included) that the embezzler not be allowed to handle the money again. To forgive the transgressor is essential; to put him or her back in the position to repeat failure might well be cruel and stupid. But these matters call for more discussion than can be offered in this little book.

However complex the subject, however difficult we find it to forgive, those who profess allegiance to Jesus Christ are called to practice forgiveness—and to practice it not because it is nice or civilized or humane, but because God in Christ has forgiven us.

# The Scarlet Letter

✦

In him we have redemption through his blood,

the forgiveness of sins, in accordance with

the riches of God's grace.

—Ephesians 1:7

Forgiveness only has meaning for those who confess there is such a thing as "wrong." (A Christian would speak of "sin," but if "wrong" is the best you can do right now, it's where you ought to begin. It isn't enough, but it's a beginning.)

There are those who hold themselves to no standard of right behavior or attitude, so they care nothing about not being forgiven. Forgiveness is a subject that has meaning only for the morally sensitive. Does that sound rather pompous? Perhaps, but I believe it's no more than the truth. When the sensitive people wrestle with the wrongs in their lives, there is a need for many things—but there is an immediate need for forgiveness. The heart that has sinned and can find no forgiveness is utterly scalded and finds life agonizing.

Though its language is rather dated now, making it a little harder for moderns to enjoy reading it, the most insightful study I know involving the need for forgiveness and the awful results of not getting it is Nathaniel Hawthorne's novel, *The Scarlet Letter.* The setting is a Puritan colony in Massachusetts, and the two leading characters are Hester Prynne and Arthur Dimmesdale. Hester has been sent ahead to America by her English husband who said he would join her soon; but more than two years pass, and she has heard not a word from him or about him.

During this time she has been immoral and eventually her shame becomes visible: she gives birth to a child. After a time in prison she is released, but the community continues to punish her by placing her periodically on a raised platform before the gaze of the whole people. Clergymen often stop her in the street and deliver sermons on the wickedness of immorality. Children follow her and call her names. In addition she must wear a dress with a large scarlet letter "A" embroidered on it which proclaims the nature of her crime. The people entreat and sometimes bully Hester to name her partner in crime, but she steadfastly refuses to do so.

One of the leaders of the community is young Arthur Dimmesdale, a capable and much-loved preacher of truth. There are sermons to be preached against such behavior, and Arthur is instructed by the elders of the community to do this while Hester sits, baby in arms, in the center of the meeting. Again and again while they are alone, Arthur begs her to reveal the name of her fellow-sinner; but she won't. It would be easier on her and only fair if she did, he tells her; but she won't reveal the name.

What the community does not know is that Arthur is her guilty partner! And he can find no peace. How can he free himself from the crushing truth? He's intelligent—will he ease the pain by burying himself in theological studies? But how can he think God's thoughts under these circumstances? He's a capable preacher—will he inspire others to live heroic and pure lives for God? But how can he inspire others to heroism while he himself is daily a coward? He's a servant—will he spend himself, humbly going from door to door to alleviate the loneliness and suffering of the needy and find peace in this way? But how can he find peace easing the burdens of others while the love of his life, having faced the wrong she has committed, suffers alone?

Dimmesdale's terrible anguish is reflected in the words of a psalmist who said about his own sin:

> When I kept silent, my bones wasted away through my groaning all day long. For day and night your hand was heavy upon me; my strength was sapped as in the heat of summer. Then I acknowledged my sin to you and did not cover up my iniquity. I said, "I will confess my transgressions to the Lord"—and you forgave the guilt of my sin.[1]

Shortly after arriving from England, Hester's husband, the harsh and relentless Roger Chillingworth, shrewdly guesses who the father is, and knowing the anguish that must exist in the heart of the preacher, asks if the preacher thinks Hester, with her scarlet letter, is more miserable than her fellow-criminal. The certain answer is that Arthur is even more miserable than Hester. In the end he joins her as an object of public shame.

The one awful omission in *The Scarlet Letter* is forgiveness. The one thing the heart cried out for and that wasn't dealt with was forgiveness. The young minister publicly confesses and dies in shame without the assurance of forgiveness. He even resists Hester's plea that he predict a reunion in heaven and urges her to remember that they broke the law.

This is not the message strugglers need to hear! While we mustn't make forgiveness a cheap passing over of wrongs, we must leave no struggler in doubt about the fullness and freeness of forgiveness. We must turn the gaze of the struggler away from his sin once it has been genuinely acknowledged, and we must speak of forgiveness. There must be no self-righteousness involved in the transaction, no impression of pomposity, no patronizing of the transgressor. There must be no, "Yes, there's full forgiveness, but only if you manifest success in your struggle against the sin you so despise."

Have none of it! Offer the sinner all the help he needs to leave his sin behind, but don't make forgiveness depend on the speed or quality of his reformation. Accept his heartfelt expressions of remorse and repentance, work with him for complete healing, but don't leave him in doubt of God's full forgiveness!

Without mercy there can be no peace for the sensitive and certainly no self-acceptance or self-respect. Join in the joy of heaven when the sinner returns seeking forgiveness. Grant it in the name of God without reservation.

# Hear the Cry I Do Not Utter

✦

When Simon Peter saw this, he fell at Jesus' knees

and said, "Go away from me, Lord;

I am a sinful man!"

—Luke 5:8

Have you ever felt the oppressive weight of darkness—a darkness that usurps your life and insinuates itself into your character and disposition? Do you sometimes fear that your heart is so hard and cold that surely God can find no place in you? Do we not sometimes actually rejoice in the darkness, revel in and sleep content in it? Darkness can blot out all thoughts of higher life; it can fill us with a sense that there is no rescue . . . and sometimes we have no desire to be rescued.

163

And yet, there comes to us the message of One who is all light and loveliness. His very presence makes us afraid of being left in darkness, enslaved and uncaring. His presence makes us feel our awful need and out of that need beg for rescue.

Louise Chandler Moulton described the confession and fear of the darkened heart when it has been stung by a sense of that presence:

> Because I seek Thee not, oh seek Thou me!
> Because my lips are dumb, oh hear the cry
> I do not utter as Thou passest by,
> And from my lifelong bondage set me free!
> Because content I perish, far from Thee,
> O seize me, snatch me from my fate, and try
> My soul in Thy consuming fire! Draw nigh
> And let me, blinded, Thy salvation see.
> If I were pouring at Thy feet my tears,
> If I were clamoring to see Thy face,
> I should not need Thee, Lord, as now I need,
> Whose dumb, dead soul knows neither hopes
> nor fears,
> Nor dreads the outer darkness of this place—
> Because I seek not, pray not, give Thou heed![1]

And isn't that how many Christians sometimes feel? Aren't we at times amazed by our lack of passion, our distorted or dim vision, the dumbness of our lips when we should be speaking to and about our Lord? Aren't we astounded at times by the fact that we couldn't care less about the world's lostness, and don't we occasionally feel almost speechless by the meanness or grossness of our sins? Aren't we tempted at such times to rip our chests open, take that pathetic little heart that pumps in there, and bring it to God with a desperate appeal: "Would you please look at this and assure me there is a place in there that has room for you?"

And don't we anguish in those moments over what he might find, or not find? Pacing up and down, looking over his shoulder while he peels back layer after layer, we wonder why it is taking so long. Is it so hard to find? Can even God find it? And what a relief, we can imagine, when he says, "Ah, there it is, the place where there is room for me."

We want to see it for ourselves; we want the assurance. We've no doubt he loves us; what we want to know is do we truly have time for him, or are we only fooling ourselves?

"Where is it?"

"There, see?"

"No, I can't, are you sure it's there?"

"Look hard. Don't you see that little area that isn't quite as dried up as the rest?"

"That's it? That's my little 'love' spot?"

"Yes!"

"What a relief. How did it get there?"

"Why, I put it there!"

By his grace, we're not so dead that we don't long to be fully alive. By his grace, we aren't so blind that we cannot see his beauty and our shabbiness. By his grace, we aren't so bound that we don't wrestle against the chains

> By his grace, we're not so dead that we don't long to be fully alive.

that would bind us. By his grace, we aren't so insensitive that we don't know what it is to long, or long to long. By his grace, if he could find no place in our diseased hearts that has room for him, we would be dismayed and would want there to be such a place.

Noted British preacher and author J. H. Jowett spoke the truth when responding to "Blessed are ye that hunger now." He said, "But suppose we do not hunger, and we know we do not? Well, we can take sides against ourselves. We can set our wills against our own desireless hearts."[2]

Yes, by God's grace, we can do at least that. Yes, there is room for God in our hearts—tiny as that room may currently be.

But even if there were no room in our hearts for God, the astounding and transforming truth is, there is room in his heart for us! And because we know that that is true, darkness has lost us. And though the night has not fully passed, those who are Christ's are "children of the day."[3] We have been called out of darkness into his marvelous light. It's just that our eyes have not yet become fully accustomed to the glory.

But our day is coming!

# Seat 15A

✦

For I will forgive their wickedness and will
remember their sins no more.

—Hebrews 8:12

I was traveling on a plane going from Atlanta to Dallas. There were still a few people on it from a previous leg of the trip, and when I got to my seat there was a man sitting there.

"Mister," I said apologetically, "I hate to disturb you, but this is my seat."

He nodded to the window seat in front of him and said, "Take that one. The plane's empty."

"It is now, but you should see the crowd that's coming on," I told him.

His wife, who was seated on the aisle, said, "Oh, take that seat." I patiently explained to her that someone would come and get me out of it saying it was theirs, so the move was now or later.

A man in the aisle, stretching his legs said, "There are lots of seats; take that one."

"Mister," I responded, "I'm having trouble enough here, please don't make it harder." And turning to the man in my seat I pleaded, "Come on, sir, let me have the seat."

Well, he got really angry, flung his stuff from the middle seat into the aisle, dragged at the stuff under the seat in front of him, and climbed out over his wife into the aisle.

I was red with embarrassment. I climbed over the wife and stuffed my little case under the seat in front of me, as she went on and on about the trouble I was creating, telling the people who were coming on how difficult and how thoughtless I was being. Then she said, "And besides, that's my husband's seat."

I had wanted to suffer in silence, but that was too much so I took out my boarding pass with 15A on it and politely but firmly told her, "No, lady, the seat is mine. See? 15A!"

Her next words killed me. "This isn't 15A!" she said.

I came to life long enough to look up in horror. I was sitting in 16A. The seat I had continued to refuse was mine! The seat I had insisted on getting was his!

Now my chest was hurting, I was sticky with sweat, and I said, "Lady, what can I tell you? I'm very sorry."

She snapped back, "You ought to be!"

I dragged out my case and dropped it into the seat in front of me, climbed out over her, and sank into my seat like water going down a waste pipe.

Humiliated, sick at my stupidity, sweating with shame, my chest hurting and my head throbbing, I sat and listened as she told the whole plane about my thoughtlessness and troublemaking, and how all along she knew it was her husband's seat. On and on she went about the kind of person I was.

I felt ill and wanted to turn to her and say, "Lady, please! If you only knew how terrible I feel over the trouble I've caused, if you only knew how you are hurting me by proclaiming my shame to everyone, you'd give me a break and leave me alone." But I couldn't, and she wouldn't turn me loose until she was quite finished.

I want you to know that *my Father isn't like that!* To those in covenant relationship with him, he promises that he will not remember their wrongs against them so as to destroy the relationship. He is not like a dog that keeps on worrying a bone.

I live in a land where we keep a detailed record of wrongs committed by the other side, as though we ourselves were free from villainy; so it isn't easy to appreciate a God who distinctly remembers forgetting.

But then, to balance things out, some of us have had the pleasure of meeting up with people who are just like God in the matter of forgiving and forgetting wrongs—people who with severe mercy deal with wrongs and are done with them—permanently! These people wouldn't dream of tormenting us with the past or spreading our shame abroad. These are the shadow of a great rock in a weary land.

I want you to know, my Father *is* like that!

# No Record of Wrongs

✦

[Love] is not rude, it is not self-seeking, it is not

easily angered, it keeps no record of wrongs.

—1 Corinthians 13:5

F our adults sat enthralled by an eleven-month-old
boy called Jason. They all hoped he was about to
take his first steps. The mother held him upright and the
father sat across from him, calling him to come to him.
The baby's grandmother watched with bated breath. His
grandfather couldn't take his eyes off him (at least in the
early stages). Everyone in the room wanted that baby to
succeed. Finally, after numerous falls without progress,

Jason took several steps unaided by anyone. The adults looked at each other in elation. They wanted to see more!

I took my eyes off Jason and watched the others for a while. My daughter, Linda, was delighted with her baby. My son-in-law, Stan, was bragging away. And my wife, Ethel, the baby's doting grandmother, couldn't get over it. What a boy! I was thrilled with my grandson. I was grateful to God that Jason was so blessed. He had people who were really committed to him. They rejoiced in his success. (They always will!) They counted each step he took on his own.

I wondered for a few minutes if they could tell me how many times he had fallen and needed to be lifted. I didn't ask; it seemed such a dumb thought. Just the same, I'm sure they couldn't have told me. They weren't counting how many times he fell; they were interested in how often he was triumphant!

I learned something that evening. I saw modeled before me the truth of Hebrews 12:1. The Hebrew writer sees the ancient worthies, as it were, urging us on, calling us to run the race well. And I saw the truth of 1 Corinthians 13:5 placarded before me: "[Love] keeps no record of wrongs."

God help us, there are too many CPAs among us, too many with accounting degrees, counting the wrongs of others. It's not that I think we should behave as doormats when others wrong us. That isn't good for the transgressors. Loving enough to confront and convict is as biblical as it is loving. No, it isn't that. It's just that for all our going on about grace, we're so sickeningly graceless. We operate so much on *numbers.* We quantify righteousness: so many good deeds done, so many evil deeds resisted; so many goods deeds not done, so many bad deeds committed. Our spiritual condition is easily determined by the number of points at the end of the columns. (I speak the truth before God when I tell you I actually possess a copy of just such a sheet circulated by certain believers for their members.)

When Peter asked Jesus if forgiving his brother seven times would be enough, Jesus told him no. "Seventy-seven times," was the response of Jesus.[1] He wasn't urging Peter to keep records; he was urging him to forget numbers.

The lady on the phone was really chewing on me: "That's the second time you've done that!" she said. The sad truth is, she was right. But it did enter my mind, as she proceeded to take my flesh off strip by strip, that two wasn't the magic number. I didn't say anything, of course, because that would have made it appear that I wasn't particularly concerned that I had done wrong. And I *was* grieved that I had done it. The facts were correct, but her spirit was wrong. The poor lady had been keeping a record of my wrongs. Love doesn't do that! I recognize this is a hard saying (especially if I'm on the receiving end of transgression). But it is the blunt saying of our Lord.

Those who care for our souls will rebuke us when necessary, but they will not keep an account of evil.

I watched the treatment Jason was receiving with pride and pleasure. I contrasted it with what is too often practiced—the ignoring of the successes and the recording of the failings. I'm happy for Jason. And I'm happy that, throughout the world, there are those who will with friendship's hand brush away the chaff in our lives and bring out for inspection the accomplishments and victories that Christ has blessed us with. And they rejoice in our successes. These friends acknowledge our mistakes.

They're saddened and often hurt by our foolishness. But they keep no record of wrongs.

What are we to do, then, with sinners who keep falling? Are we talking about sinners like ourselves? What do we do with ourselves? I know myself better than I know anyone else in the world (and I don't know me very well). And I know that beyond my general "decency" and my ceaseless longing to make God proud of me, to please him and make him smile, beyond that is a sinner whose life isn't even *remotely* like Christ's.

What am I to do with little Jason? Pretend he isn't in need of daily cleansing and help? Encourage him to compare the "numbers" in his life with the numbers in someone else's? Threaten to disown him because of his failures? Urge him to keep an account of the wrongs of others so he won't notice his own? I suppose that's possible, but then where is the poor little man? If I isolate him because of his poor numbers, then what happens to the undying drive within him to really live and live for God? Do I dismiss all that with, "Sorry, but no cigar"?

Do you know what I think? I think that only lovers can really make sense of someone else's life. If anyone has the right to lecture Jason for his falls, it would have to be those who loved him, those who are right in there with him, prepared to pay for the privilege. But these people are too much in love with him to even think of lectures.

There is One who sees us all for what we are rather than what we think we are or even *wish* we were. And would you believe it, he won't keep a record of wrongs.[2]

What was that you said? "Yes, but . . ."?

# The Toys

✦

"In a surge of anger I hid my face from you for a
moment, but with everlasting kindness
I will have compassion on you,"
says the Lord your Redeemer.
—Isaiah 54:8

Believe me when I tell you that I'm not interested in minimizing sin—not yours or mine. I know all the verses, I have some idea of what the Cross of Christ says about our sin, and I can become as infuriated as the next person when someone undoubtedly guilty seems to get away with something. When it comes to sin, I know it's important that we take God's side even against ourselves.

None of that is especially noble or profound. We all feel this way, don't we? We don't want our sin whitewashed.

But the Cross must be allowed its full implications. God knew us to be sinners from the beginning; no one needed to lecture him about our evil. He alone in all the universe takes it with the utmost seriousness—and still he loves us. The Cross didn't create the love of God for sinners; it manifested it, made it known in a way that defies full comprehension.

However maddening our own sin or the sin of others is to us, we aren't given permission to make sin say more than the Cross! The Cross speaks louder than sin! Where sin shouts, the Cross thunders; where evil increases, grace in the Cross increases more and deals with it all; where sin whispers its lies and confuses us, the Cross heralds its truth and drives away the darkness.

God pities us! He sees us as not only sinners but as sinned against. He has a heart full of compassion, a heart eager beyond words to forgive us. We mustn't keep that truth from people, no matter what evil they've done.

Yes, we're tired of people taking advantage of us (God, too, of course) and want it stopped. Yes, we're sometimes afraid that forgiveness will encourage people to remain in their sin (though we don't often think that of ourselves and our own sin). But while those feelings may be understandable, they're no excuse for denying the truth about God's love of all transgressors and his hunger—yes, hunger!—to bring them into fulness of life with him.

**God sees us as not only sinners but as sinned against.**

Coventry Patmore, an English poet of several generations ago, wrote "The Toys,"[1] a poem about a little boy who got into trouble with his father, was punished, and sent to bed unkissed. This child, "his mother who was patient, being dead" struggled alone to his bedroom with heart breaking, less at the punishment as at his father's disappointment and the emotional gulf that had appeared. The father, reflecting on the situation, says:

> Then, fearing lest his grief should hinder sleep,
> I visited his bed,
> But found him slumbering deep,
> With darkened eyelids, and their lashes yet
> From his late sobbing wet.
> And I, with moan,
> Kissing away his tears, left others of my own;
> For, on a table drawn beside his head,
> He had put, within his reach,
> A box of counters and a red-veined stone,
> A piece of glass abraded by the beach,
> And six or seven shells,
> A bottle with bluebells,
> And two French copper coins, ranged there with
>     careful art,
> To comfort his sad heart.

Even the stern theologian P. T. Forsyth—who had strong things to say about a religion that stresses too much the love of God and makes "the Father a banker for a spendthrift race"[2]—even he remarks that this poem "melts us, it is very sacred."[3] Is there a father anywhere, worthy of the name, who does not feel the pain of this father? And knowing that if we being evil can feel such love and compassion toward our erring children, should we suppose that God would not feel such feelings about his?

Did Christ not make that kind of argument when wanting to assure his timid followers of God's commitment to them? "If you, then, though you are evil, know how to give good gifts to your children, how much more will your Father in heaven give good gifts to those who ask him!"[4]

Patmore drew that conclusion and went on to close his poem with this:

> When Thou rememberest of what toys
> We made our joys,
> How weakly understood
> Thy great commanded good,
> Then, fatherly not less
> Than I whom Thou hast moulded out of clay,
> Thou'lt leave Thy wrath, and say,
> "I will be sorry for their childishness."

Too sentimental? Too soft? Yes, the fatherhood of God must be seen in the light of the Cross which expresses his hatred of sin, and it is right to be reminded that if God is a father he is to be honored.[5] But a psalmist insists that God does not treat us as our sins deserve, that he will not always be accusing us, that he will have pity on us and remove our sins from us as far as the east is from the west "for he knows how we are formed, he remembers that we are dust."[6]

For those who set their hearts to please God and run for refuge to his Christ, there is assurance of full forgiveness. Our own attempts at full forgiveness are, at their ultimate best, pitiable and wavering, a mere shadow of the fathomless depths of God's own forgiving grace. To obscure the truth that God is absolutely delighted at the opportunity to wipe out the sins of those who've run to him for refuge is a crime not only against fear-filled strugglers, it is a slander against God himself.[7]

# Bethlehem's Well

✦

Oh, that someone would get me a drink of water
from the well near the gate of Bethlehem!

—2 Samuel 23:15

What's the big deal about Bethlehem water?
Water's just water, after all.

Is it indeed?

David had been warned off this well as a child and had played around it as a boy. He'd drawn water from it for his family, gossiped there with his friends after a long day's work, and grown fondly accustomed to the slightly distinctive taste of that water (a distinction that would tend to grow as memory looked back on it). He might even

179

have remembered some days, said W. E. Beck, "when the drawing and the drudgery had rasped on his nerves, and he had cursed the dear old well, and voted it a nuisance; but now, 'Oh, that someone would get me a drink of water from the well near the gate of Bethlehem.' "[1]

"Water's just water" indeed. Might as well say a house is just a house or a tree is just a tree or a river is just a river.

David was now a warrior, a veteran of a hundred engagements and able to draw to him tough, war-hardened legionaires. But for all his capacity for ruthlessness and hand-to-hand combat, there were times when his mind followed his heart back to home—home as it had been in innocent days. Days when the driving thought was nothing more than a long cool drink for a parched throat after a day with the sheep. That would be enough; he'd be content with that! Days when he slept secure and wouldn't have nightmares about a man called Uriah or be terrorized by the thought of God as he watched a man called Uzzah dying at his feet.

Now he was, perhaps, an outlaw king, living away from home in the hills among the ravines. There was no shortage of water where he was, but as he licked his dry lips, his thoughts flew like a bird down the gorges and over the hills to the place of innocence and carefree pleasure—Bethlehem, his hometown with its sweet old well.

Three friends saw the dream in his eyes and heard his whispered request, murmured to no one but himself. And because they loved him so, off they went on the short but difficult journey to that place, now surrounded by Philistine troops. They fought their way through those guarding the well and plunged the skin into the cold water far below. They fought their way back to freedom and raced back with their prize to their astonished leader and friend.

To his everlasting credit David saw such devotion as too pure and too deep for a mere mortal to accept. That kind of devotion should be given only to God, he thought, so he poured the water out in a sacrifice to God.

Well done, David! Very well done!

There are times when we are fed up with our crabby hearts and peevish ways. We reflect in a wave of nostalgia —but more than that—on the days of innocence that are gone; days when we weren't so cunning, so super-sensitive, so concerned about our reputation; days when we were pleased to settle for less and didn't think it any sacrifice; days when we faced life with eagerness and helpfulness; days when our trust was simpler and life wasn't a giant puzzle to be solved; days when we smiled easily, ate with pleasure, and slept peacefully.

And in our remorse, in our sense of loss, in our feeling that we have wandered far from home, we murmur, "Oh, that someone would get me a drink of water from the well near the gate of Bethlehem."

There is other water of course. We can drink at other wells. There's no shortage of water vendors. But there's nothing like the water from the well at Bethlehem.

And in answer to our silent prayer—in answer to the unspoken prayer of the human race—a Friend, who hears what we did not say and couldn't ask, makes the danger-ous journey and, at great cost, fights his way past the enemy who had claimed the well, and he brings back the water of salvation.

In a moment of insight, seized by the unutterable glory and grace of it all, we're tempted to say, "Oh, but that's too much for me to accept; that must surely be given to God alone."

And he says he did it for God and that it is the glory

and good pleasure of God that we receive it. The way to receive the gift, he insists, is to take it into our lives and pour our lives out before God as offerings.

Even seasoned warriors for Christ wake up sometimes to find themselves far from home, far from the spirit and sounds of home, the looks and dreams of home, the memories and purposes of home. They involve themselves in things of which they should be ashamed and forget what the Voice said to Thompson, "All things betray thee, who betrayest Me." [2]

How glorious a truth it is that when we from our hearts murmur that prayer, "Oh, that someone would get me a drink of water from the well near the gate of Bethlehem," and behold, a tall, cool, crystal-clear glass of water appears before us. Cool and pure and good. This water eases our hot fevered souls and brings life and refreshment to our weary spirits—sick with their wandering, in need of forgiveness and renewal.

How fine it is of God to get us water from the well at Bethlehem.

# Behold the Woman

✦

For I desire mercy, not sacrifice,

and acknowledgment of God

rather than burnt offerings.

—Hosea 6:6

The crowd parted to let them through. A group of upright men and their victim—a woman caught in the very act of adultery. She was under the condemnation not only of her harsh and hypocritical accusers, she was under the condemnation of the healthiest morality, the divine law itself. But though that's true, that's not the central concern of John 8:1–11.

The danger in being an accuser (perhaps a *mere* accuser) is that we're tempted to believe there are two classes—the guilty and the innocent. We're tempted to think we're in the innocent class and the other is in the guilty class. The particular sin under review was committed by another, not us, so we're tempted to forget that at the very moment of judging, we, too, are guilty sinners. If we buckle to that temptation, we ignore God's word of judgment against ourselves and walk in danger.

Bonhoeffer was right. The Word of God in Jesus Christ pronounces us guilty, even when we don't feel guilty. And it pronounces us not guilty, even when we don't feel righteous.

And Pascal only tells us the truth when he reminds us there is only one class before God—the guilty. There are only the righteous who believe they are sinners and the sinners who believe they are righteous.

To isolate this woman's particular sin was to deal with sins one at a time. Their view of sin and themselves led them to "keep score" and come out looking good. But what if he who knows all were to pull *them* up short every time they sinned? What if their sins—ranging from attitudes to words to deeds, sins of omission as well as commission, sins that were momentary expressions of their overall sinfulness—what if each one was brought up and examined? What then?

As Christ wipes away the sin that the woman shamefully acknowledges, he brings to light, to conviction, the sin her accusers don't acknowledge and won't confess. They may have gone off in frustration, muttering objections and jibes like, "He's soft on sin," but they carried their burden of sin away with them. Their turn for absolution would come only when they confessed they were blind. Then he would give them sight.

But on this sinner—dumb with shame under accusations she can't refute—Christ pronounces God's word of absolution. He doesn't deny her sin, doesn't minimize it, doesn't ignore it, doesn't parade or proclaim it; he absolves it! And in drawing this woman close to his heart and standing with her against her accusers, the Master puts his own reputation at risk.

Sometimes we feel obliged to "protect" God's honor by condemning the sinner. But no one honored God more than Christ did. No one was more concerned that God be honored than Jesus was. Yet he never gave the impression that either he or his Father were consumed with thoughts of their own honor. In dealing with sinners, Christ behaved honorably and never at his Father's expense.

Christ was able to absolve the woman's guilt because he was bearing it already on his heart and would bear it in his body upon the tree. The word of absolution wasn't cheap because it cost God his Son and the Son his life, poured out in an atoning death.

The judgment of the Pharisees, on the other hand, was cheap because they stood apart from her, distancing themselves from her evil. In doing this, their uprightness became corruption and their goodness rotted their souls.

Jesus went on to verbally forbid the woman's sin, because in absolving her sin he was not ignoring it or approving it. It really did need bearing, it really did need forgiving. Since it was contrary to the heart of God, he opposed it and plainly said so.

But he didn't say that to the crowd or the preachers—he said it to the woman. Another risky move! In the presence of the upright, he was pleased to align himself with the sinner until they physically distanced themselves from her by walking away. Had he distanced himself from her, knowing something of the grand sweep of his life and his way with people, we would have been disappointed. More than that, dismayed—terrified, maybe. Because in our saner moments we all see ourselves as the woman in the spotlight.

How great the temptation is to the upright to put a moral space between themselves and the transgressor. The righteous "troubleshooters" were there to guard God's majesty, to save Israel's name, don't you see. So for the very best reasons they themselves couldn't forgive her in private; they had to make an example of her, had to spread the news about her. It wouldn't do for the word to get around that they hadn't "dealt with it," that Israel, under their leadership, was soft on sin.

It never occurred to them to hide her shame from others while they dealt with it. Never occurred to them that if her sin had become known they could have stood by her and said, "Yes! We knew. We dealt with it, and we noted her repentance and remorse. What more did you want? You want more than that? Then read the scandal sheets. Proclaiming shame is their business, not ours."

Another danger in being a (mere) accuser is that we distance ourselves from penitent people at the time when they are most vulnerable. For the sensitive, there are few places more lonely than in the spotlight of moral judgment.

In relation to her accusers, the woman was in a position where no matter what, she couldn't win. She could never have said: "I tried to resist. God help me; it seems to be a war that never ends. Just when I thought I was safe, when I thought I finally had things the right way up, he came along and everything fell apart. You think my shame began today when you caught me? My shame has been my food for so long. Perhaps you don't know what it is to struggle with evil in the way I do. You people have won your way through to uprightness."

But there was someone there who could speak words for her. When he said, "Why don't you turn the spotlight of God on yourselves?" their grip on her was broken and his grip on her was strengthened.

They meant it for evil; God meant it for good. The pain she helped bring on herself served God's purposes. She sinned, humbled herself, and God came and stood by her side. As a result, penitent sinners down the centuries—behind faces burning with embarrassment—feel there is still reason to go on. Through her sin and her being shamed, we have an eternal record of what God did in Christ for sinners. Her sin served God!

Yes, yes, I know sin is sin! There aren't many things more tedious than discussions that go on and on proving something that no one in his right mind would dispute. The issue is not, Is sin involved? but What are we to do about it? How are we to respond to it? How can we help? and What precisely is our obligation?

The incident involving this woman caught in sin doesn't cover all the ground that needs to be covered in dealing with sin, but they are foolish who don't take a long look at this portrait of God and a long look at their own sin, motives, and methods.

SIX

# CALLING

It's said that after Mother
Teresa received the Nobel Peace
Prize, she was approached by
some reporters. They asked her
if such acclaim and recognition
might not go to her head. In
response, she asked them if they
remembered the story of
Christ's entering Jerusalem on a
donkey and the road being
strewn with garments and palm
branches by the adoring crowd.
They said they did. She replied,
"And do you think the donkey
thought it was in his honor?"

✦

# The Incomparable One

◆

Who alone is immortal and who lives
in unapproachable light, whom no one has
seen or can see. To him be honor and
might forever. Amen.

—1 Timothy 6:16

Holiness speaks of "difference," "otherness," "not
the sameness," "separation." When the Bible
speaks of God, we learn he is holy because he is like no
other god, because his glory, majesty, and purity separate
him from all else that exists. These qualities and his
attributes mean he is incomparable, in a class by himself.

In one of the books from C. S. Lewis's *Chronicles of
Narnia,* Shasta finally meets up with Aslan, and with awe
approaching dread, asks him, "Who are you?" Aslan three

times answers, "Myself!" First in a low rumble that shook the ground. Then in a tone of gaiety as though perfectly content with who he was. And finally in a whisper so low you had to strain to hear, and yet it seemed to come from everywhere.[1] "Myself!" Like no one or nothing else. Not simply different, but different because of the inexpressible wonder of his person! Isn't that what Isaiah said? "To whom will you compare me or count me equal? To whom will you liken me that we may be compared?"[2]

In the case of objects, places, times, and people that are "holy to the Lord," these have been invested with *difference.* They have been called out from ordinary (profane) use, service, or status and have been separated unto God and to his purposes. It's that divine call, that divine initiative, that makes them holy.

If God claims a particular piece of turf, it becomes holy, and it will be entered or walked on only under certain conditions. If it's a spot close to a burning bush, the worshiper will go barefoot on that spot. If it's a mountain, it will be roped off and transgressors threatened. If we're thinking of spoons, pots, dishes, and the like, they will be used only for the service laid out by the God who makes them holy. If it is money or gifts of another kind, it and they will be used only to promote the glory and purposes of the God to whom they are given. If it's a period of time, it is differentiated from the rest of time and certain prescribed behavior (or lack of it) will mark it out as different (holy). If it is a person—a priest, perhaps—that one will be separated by God from other people and given responsibilities and privileges that are peculiar to him.

When it is a people (a nation) who have been made holy, they become, by their separation, a different people.

As with everything we've mentioned, this people will no longer be the same, and this "not the sameness" will be marked out. It will be made visible by certain rituals or patterns of behavior, certain convictions held, certain stories told, certain visions for the future, and certain perspectives on the past and present. Having been made different, they can no longer be the same as the rest of the people.

Let me repeat, this God of the Bible is holy by virtue of simply being what he is, by just being himself! His holiness is underived, his own person creates the notion of holiness. Everything else either flows from him as the fountain of holiness or stands over against him as counterfeit.

We who belong to God have already been made holy by his counsel. We are called again and again to live out that already existing holiness. We are to live up to our calling, as Paul put it.[3] And Peter said we are to live as "obedient children" and to be holy in life since "he who called you is holy."[4] And since we have embraced as Father one who judges the lives of people righteously, we are to live our lives in reverent fear.[5]

The Old Testament tirelessly proclaims the same truth: "I am the Lord your God, who has set you apart from the nations. . . . You are to be holy to me because I, the Lord, am holy, and I have set you apart from the nations to be my own."[6] This holy God chose and sanctified (separated) Israel and now calls them to live that holiness out in a glad-hearted allegiance to him in ways that reflects his image.

The Hebrew writer reminds his readers that they are holy[7] and share in a heavenly calling. Later he insists that chastisement from God is meant to make them sharers in the holiness of God[8] and calls them to pursue holiness if they wish to see God.[9]

This is the consistent approach to holiness in the Bible, Old Testament and New Testament. Paul urged Corinthian believers to purge "leaven" from the assembly that they might become what they already are, unleavened.[10] Peter constantly reminded his readers that they were what they were as a result of God's activity on their behalf; and because they were what they were, they should live out what they were—a people separated not only *from* something but *unto* something and Someone.

These were the people of Aslan—the Incomparable One.

# Is Nothing Sacred?

✦

Since everything will be destroyed in this way,
what kind of people ought you to be?
You ought to live holy and godly lives.
—2 Peter 3:11

I'm wanting to confess the need for more reminders, more tangible reminders, that I am holy and should be pursuing holiness. When I mention this to my friends, I discover that many of them feel the same need.

I have the settled conviction that we're too cerebral for our own good. In the Old Testament there were a million things that reminded people of holiness. A million actions, words, gestures, places, times, and objects that were useful in the pursuit of holiness. Many modern

Christians dismiss such things too quickly and too easily. Holiness is a thing of the mind, a thing of the thought processes, they say. Holiness is a disposition; it's intangible; it's an attitude; and everyone knows that physical acts, postures, gestures, places, times, and objects have nothing to do with the inner world. I hear a lot of that. We've outgrown the Old Testament; we're very modern and much more sophisticated than the ancient believers. What do we need with things that prompt us to holiness?

Because we know that God doesn't dwell in buildings made with hands and that "the church is the people and not the building," we're inclined to dismiss all talk of holy places, clothing, and furniture as dispensational ignorance. We're sure that people who need such things are mere children. Besides, there's always the danger of formalism and ceremonialism setting in.

**Because we know that God doesn't dwell in buildings made with hands, we're inclined to dismiss all talk of holy places as dispensational ignorance.**

But maybe the Old Testament saints knew God didn't dwell in houses made with hands; maybe they knew that he wasn't confined to a specific location. (Didn't I read that somewhere in Solomon's temple dedication speech, and didn't I hear Isaiah rebuke the people who thought they could bribe God into helping them by promising to build him a fine house?) So if they knew God wouldn't and couldn't be confined to a geographical spot, maybe there's more to their talk of holy places, clothing, furniture, and periods of time than we modern believers have taken into account.

And we can't be ignorant of the fact that the Old Testament is filled with warnings against mere bowing, gesturing, fasting, and the like—outward trappings of religion that lacked heart or were offered as substitutes for obedience at the social, ethical, and spiritual level. I don't think we need to lecture Old Testament prophets on the dangers of outward observance; they are our major teachers in these matters.

To treat the Old Testament as a carnival of ceremonial actions with some good historical illustrations thrown in as sermon helps is an outrage at worst and pathetic at best. We've gotten the impression that because the New Testament sometimes speaks of Old Testament truths as being "shadows" of things to come"[1] that it somehow lacks spiritual substance. That's not what the New Testament writers were getting at when they spoke of "shadow" truths. The idea that the Old Testament is graceless, legalistic, or not really spiritual is another serious blunder that robs the church and the world of what they can't afford to lose.

So, freed from any sense of "holy space," we build our basketball courts (often literally) next door to the auditorium where we gather to praise, pray, listen, and commune. Our young adults and children often come in sweating and panting, at the last minute, in time to engage in prayer and listening to God. And how can we critique it? We have no holy times or spaces. Everything is holy, even the basketball court. Right?

I would like to think I don't need promptings to remind me to pursue holiness—but I do. I would like to think I can (characteristically) slip into a holiness mood just by an exertion of the mind, a mental choosing, rather than being shaped by habit, ritual, and countless prompters—but I can't. As it appears to me, the church of God, in general, thinks it can stroll its way into holiness, or that without preparation it can bustle into God's holy presence—but it can't.

We sometimes talk as though we invented the notion that God is everywhere. Didn't the psalmist complain about that very truth—that he couldn't get away from God?[2] Old Testament saints had no problem with combining the truth that God could be anywhere with the truth that God graciously manifested himself to and communed with sinners in specific places.

Because we know the building isn't the church, we think we know the building isn't a special place; and because we think the building isn't a special place, we have no special place. "Ah, but every place is special," we're told, "and it's precisely for this reason that the New Testament will have no regard for the holiness of special locations." This is another shallow understanding of the New Testament teaching. Not even we believe that. Sleeping attire in a bedroom is totally appropriate, but pajamas at a Communion assembly?

We have a place built into our building complex to make coffee and tea, to play basketball or dominoes, and to eat meals—but where is the place reserved for those who would like to spend some time in prayer? There's no room marked "For Prayer Only." There's no place where we can't make jokes, talk about the weather, munch on our donuts, and slurp our coffee. The sense of the holy is driven out by the impression that nowhere is holy, everything is equally profane or holy. But who are we kidding? Professing that everything is equally holy doesn't, in practice, elevate our sense of the holy; it brings it down. The lack of holy places, times, or ritual allows us to drift into a generalized profanity where nothing is sacred.

We are even able to look at one another—the elect of God, a holy nation, and a kingdom of priests—unaware of who is before us. Going beyond the blessed truth that we're all fellow-heirs in Christ, we can treat those who lead and feed us in the most disgraceful and derisive manner. As though the place God has given them as his ministers means nothing. Where did we learn this?

We don't want our assemblies (or our lives) to be stuffy, stagnant, rigid, gloomy, suffocatingly predictable or anything like that. But is there not the need for many of them to be less laid back, less consumer-oriented, less entertaining, less "movin' and shakin'," less "friendly" toward God? I think many of us are killing ourselves by breezing into his presence with a jaunty wave in his direction, "Well, you know why we're here, Pal." We do need to celebrate, but there's a need to "rejoice with trembling."[3]

It can't be right to have people cower before him, slavishly afraid of him. Not since Bethlehem, not since Golgotha! It can't be right to withhold grace and joy from his people or to lead them to be uncertain about his utter commitment to them.

But it can't be wrong to reverence God. It can't be wrong to stop sometimes, made speechless by the almost incredible grace of it all that we should even be allowed into his presence. This grace is stunning and breathtaking; and it required Bethlehem, Gethsemane, and Golgotha. To enter our assemblies to worship as if it were a right we've grown accustomed to—to do that—that is breathtaking.

# The Key

✦

We also rejoice in our sufferings, because we know
that suffering produces perseverance; perseverance,
character; and character, hope.

—Romans 5:3–4

I n Tuscumbia, Alabama, in 1870 the Keller's baby girl
fell ill, and this resulted in her becoming blind, deaf,
and mute. She was nineteen months old. Without com-
munication she grew into a "little human animal,"
trapped in the silent darkness, a victim to moods and to
the ways her sad parents spoiled her because they didn't
know what else to do. "Every day she slips further and
further away," said her mother, "and I don't know how to
call her back."

Then Annie Sullivan arrived. She wasn't much more than a child herself, but she had known real life and all the pain, frustration, and heartache that goes with it. But her suffering had taught her toughness as well as compassion.

She isn't long at the Keller's before Helen shows her that she knows the power of a key—she locks Sullivan in her room so she can't trouble her anymore. Annie, realizing that she can't help Helen because the parents continue to interfere with her work with the girl, asks them to let her have complete control over the child, in a little summer house next to the main house.

They take Helen for a long drive so she won't know where she is, they deposit her in the summer house, and they leave immediately. By now Helen regards Sullivan as her tormentor, so you can imagine her horror when she realizes she is left alone with someone who will give her no peace. In panic, she tries to find the door, to escape the clutches of this one who refuses to let her do as she wishes; but when she finds it, it's locked, and the woman has the key. Locked in by sightless eyes and unhearing ears, she's now locked in with her torturer.

For two weeks Sullivan "torments" Helen, refusing to let her eat or sleep or play unless she is willing to abide by the rules. She tirelessly teaches her the letters of the alphabet on her hands, trying to get through to her that words stand for things, that things have names, and that the shapes made by her fingers and hands are the letters that spell the names that stand for the things.

Two weeks fly by without a breakthrough. The parents can no longer stand the separation and resist Sullivan's pleas for more time. They take Helen back—prison's ended; torment's over; she's free again.

As soon as she's back in the house, she goes around

checking all the doors to see that they're unlocked, and then she takes the key and puts it in her mother's pocket, making sure that her tormentor won't have power over her again. All the obedience and rules she has learned are tossed to the winds and the animal behavior returns. Finally, it all comes to a head when Helen throws a jug of water over the teacher. Sullivan ignores the protests of the parents, grabs the jug and Helen, drags her out to the pump, forces her to fill the jug with water while she spells W..A..T..E..R on the girl's fingers and hands.

And that's when it happens. All of a sudden Helen stops struggling. She throws away the jug and allows the water to run through her fingers as she strains to say the one word she had learned when she was a nineteen-month-old baby: water! The light comes on in her mind, she struggles to understand that what was being spelled out on her fingers stands for what she feels pouring over her hands. Her prison walls are collapsing; she now has a rational connection with her world—*words* are *things.*

Afraid to believe, in case she's mistaken, she makes Sullivan pump more water, feels it, grabs her teacher's hand, and spells out WATER? The teacher confirms it and slowly the tears begin to flow as freedom steals into her life. Ecstatically, she wants to know the name of everything—the word for what's under her feet, for the soil she can pick up in her hands, for the thing the water comes out of. The father and mother join the celebration and there's crying and laughing as the girl communicates with the world around her and learns the name "Mother."

All of a sudden, she turns from her parents, finds Sullivan, and asks her what her name is. Sullivan spells out "teacher." Softness and gratitude spread over Helen's face. She stumbles her way back to her mother, who holds her and doesn't want to let her go; but Helen, groping for the key in her mother's pocket, gets it and wriggles free. Back she goes to the teacher, opens her hand, and presses the key into it. Now she knows! Now she trusts! All along her tormentor had been her friend; the one who had been locking her in was wanting to set her free.

What she'd needed all her life, unknown to her, was someone who would do less or more for her; she needed someone who would demand things of her, who would put her through some pain in order to right the wrong and change her world.

And when we, by the grace of God, awake to discover that God's laws are not meant to narrow us, not meant to cheat us, not meant to bind us, when we discover that they are meant to set us free, enrich our lives, and deepen us as people—when we discover that—like Helen Keller, we'll beg for more discipline, more "rules," and more life.

The gulf that existed between the silent, isolated world of the earlier Helen and the one she came to know can hardly be measured. The gulf that exists between our grimy, self-centered, unholy world and that one to which God calls us is beyond measure.

Helen didn't know, couldn't know, that she needed the training that Sullivan subjected her to. Even if she had known, she might not have been willing to pay the price for the reward, since she could have no real understanding of what that reward would mean.

Our own blindness and deafness, while rarely complete, can be so marked that we have little understanding of our need for discipline. And it's a lack of that training in righteousness that is so much of our problem. We need to be practiced in holiness; we need to be disciplined and shaped and held accountable.

We don't know what we're missing!

Our own inability to grasp the beauty and freedom of a rich world of purity, kindness, and guilt-free joy must surely keep us from pursuing it with the eagerness of starving men in search of food.

Once in a while, we gasp in amazement at our capacity to revel in filth and gorge ourselves with the putrid. Now and then we stand astonished at how cruel and thoughtless we can be. In a moment of insight, as when a flash of lightning illuminates an unfamiliar place, showing us the direction we are to go—in that passing moment, we catch sight of who we ought and want to be. How precious those moments are!

Flashes of insight are God-sent, but they aren't enough. We need training, discipline, and those who love us enough to ask more of us than we sometimes care to give.

# "Be Holy"

✦

Be imitators of God, therefore,

as dearly loved children.

—Ephesians 5:1

We ask too little. God help us, we ask too little. I know that in my bones!

Tyranny is terrible, but in a culture that just about worships freedom and has infected the church with a rampant individualism, most of us aren't in danger of being tyrannized. We settle for less not only because we've failed so much and have been disheartened, but because the call to holiness has been watered down and therapy has replaced the proclamation of God's purposes.

I know from personal experience how difficult it is to maintain a balance here. One moment I find myself "understanding" too easily my sinfulness and the sins of others, and then again I find myself uncompromisingly harsh with myself and others who are weak and vulnerable. At times, I wish to proclaim the power of sin even in the life of Christians, and then I hear the call of God in Scripture that implies we have strength I haven't even begun to tap. On one hand, I feel sickened by our rebellion and shallowness, and on the other, I am startled by God's faith in us that leads him to say, "Surely they are my people, sons who will not be false to me."[1]

Is our present state of moral and spiritual weakness all we should expect? If it is, then let's face up to it and stop calling one another to unreasonable heights of holiness. Let's admit we're maggots that crawl about in a dung-heap world. Let's stop tormenting ourselves and others with ringing words of challenge as if we could really climb those heights. Let's just enjoy our slop and thank God that he is willing to accept us just as we are—morally and spiritually degraded.

But we rebel against the very thought of that, don't we? We want more than pardon, we want glorious holiness. In our better moments, our higher moments, we damn the sin that so easily has its way with us. We denounce every false way, renounce the sins of the flesh, disposition, and spirit, and bitterly curse ourselves for the shallowness and apathy that seem to thrive in our very tissues.

And in those periods when we're lamenting how pathetic we are, there's a real temptation to self-pity, which only compounds the problem. But he who knows us best, who knows perfectly the depths of our weakness, startles us—us, can you believe it?—by calling us to "Be holy, because I am holy."[2]

Has he not seen how often we've been beaten? Does he not know the depths of depravity in which we have been schooled as children? Does he not see the sea of indifference in which we swim? How can he miss the fact that we struggle along alone, with precious little help from those who are supposed to love us in Christ? Is he not aware how hard it is for humans to stand strong against powerful foes within and without? Does he not know when he's flogging a dead horse? The mass of us are pathetic failures, and the best of us are hardly much better.

But paint it as we will, lament all we want, dither between extremes as we might, he will not let us alone. "Be holy, because I am holy."

And it's that call, coming from Scripture, coming from exceptional lives, coming from the matchless life of Jesus, coming from God himself, that continues to haunt us. It's all that, that in the end makes us impatient with those who want to wrap us up in cotton and overprotect us. It's because God has infiltrated us that so many of us can't settle for slime or moral mediocrity. We'd rather be tormented with lovely longings not yet realized than tamely sink without a trace into moral dullness.

**We'd rather be tormented with lovely longings not yet realized than tamely sink without a trace into moral dullness.**

Yes, and there's a price to pay for this. A certain restlessness that means we can't always be as happy as "the happy pagan." But it's a price worth paying, because where God is at work in our hearts, we can only love the highest when we see it. It's this that makes the Christian's confession of sin all the more poignant. We know what we're called to be, and comparing that to what we are, we sometimes anguish over the failure.

> [We] know that as long as life lasts we must fall short of our aims, and yet there abides in the depths of our souls the vision we can't forsake, which attracts, comforts, and strengthens even when it condemns. One thing we may not do. We may not be content with anything less than the ideal.[3]

And that means we may not, and by God's grace we will not, allow ourselves to be talked into despair of the outcome because he who gave us the hunger will fill us. The unceasing call, "Be holy," implies that we can. He wouldn't say, "Be holy because I am holy," if it were not possible for us. He would not speak to a corpse and say "Live" unless he were giving the power of life!

# The Image of the Christ

✦

But for you who revere my name, the sun of
righteousness will rise with healing in its wings.
And you will go out and leap like calves
released from the stall.

—Malachi 4:2

Only now and then do I think of it, and even then,
not too seriously. I think how much they miss
who live in areas that don't have the seasons clearly
defined. How fine it is after a long winter—when everything looks so dead that we might be tempted to think
there never will be life again—how fine it is that spring
comes.

And so it is as we look at the barrenness in our lives—
long in the grip of winter, desolate, and unpromising.

Then Jesus comes, and our desolate world bursts into life. Hopeless, sinful, and rejected, we feel the sun rising in our hearts, feel our souls warming, feel the icy grip of death and barrenness slackening and life stealing into every corner of our being.

Born again!

Homer Rodeweaver got it right when he gave us this hymn:

> One sat alone
> Beside a highway begging,
> His eyes were blind
> The light he could not see.
> He clutched his rags
> And shivered in the shadows,
> Then Jesus came
> And bade his darkness flee.
> When Jesus comes
> The tempter's power is broken,
> When Jesus comes
> The tears are wiped away.
> He takes the gloom
> And fills the life with glory,
> For all is changed
> When Jesus comes to stay.[1]

That's how it begins—our life of holiness, our life lived in the presence of God. But it's only the beginning, because God continues his creative work, transforming us more and more into the image of the Christ we received into our lives. We're grateful for pardon and amazed at forgiveness; yet, because God would have it so and enables us to feel this way, we want more—we want holiness, beauty, and richness of life. We want more than his gifts; we want his likeness. And though it may take a lifetime before we feel assured that we've made sure progress, we don't despair in the quest for holiness that God has placed within our hearts—for he is faithful who called us, and he will complete it.[2]

James S. Stewart, noted Scottish preacher and friend of the famous William Barclay, tells us there was once in the city of Florence a massive, shapeless block of marble that seemed fitted to be the raw material of some colossal statue. One sculptor after another tried his hand at it, without success. They cut and carved and hewed and chipped at it, till it seemed hopelessly disfigured.

Then someone suggested they give Michelangelo a shot at it. He began by having a house built right over the block of marble, and for long months he was shut up there with it, nobody knowing what he was doing. Then one day he flung open the door and told them to come in. They did, and there before their eyes—instead of a shapeless, meaningless block—was the magnificent statue of David, one of the glories of the world. So it is that Christ takes defeated and disfigured lives and refashions them into the very image of God.[3]

Does it take long? Will it involve the chisel and the hammer? Will we not wish now and then that God would put up with less and leave us simply "decent"? Leave us with disfigurement. Leave us with unconfronted bitterness, unbridled ambition, hypersensitivity, uncleanness, and some desire to pursue our own agendas. Will we not now and then prefer to be left less shaped, will we not wish our "Michelangelo" were less demanding?

Probably. But if marble could feel and think and know, would it—having seen itself a shapeless, disfigured mass with incredible potential and then later as the *David*—would it regret the process? Would it want to go back and have it all undone?

And so it is, one day we will catch a glimpse of a lovely creature that fills our heart with admiration and pleased astonishment. Imagine our amazement when we discover that the lovely creature is ourself—in the image of the Christ!

The beauty of holiness is our inheritance.

♦

# Too Much Like "Saints"?

✦

You are a chosen people, a royal priesthood, a holy
nation, a people belonging to God, that you may
declare the praises of him who called you out of
darkness into his wonderful light.

—1 Peter 2:9

Sarah wasn't sure how she should act. Though she
was a Christian she knew what it was to struggle
with sin in her life. In fact, if the truth were told, she
seemed to struggle more with sin now than she did when
she wasn't a Christian. But she knew this was, at least in
part, because she had a better vision of how life could and
should be lived. Before she met Christ, it didn't matter
much what she thought or did; but now, how could she
not be more sensitive to what was unlike Christ?

The people she worked with were no worse but no better than what she had been, and while a lot of what went on in the office grieved her, she didn't want to come across as a "saint." The temptation to be less than what she felt God had called her to be was strong. She didn't always want to be "different." But the reason she didn't want to appear different was because she didn't feel her life was sufficiently clean and devoted to Christ. At times she thought, "I'm no better than they are. How can I stand in judgment of them without being self-righteous and hypocritical?"

I don't find that hard to understand. I have experienced and do even now experience similar emotions; but, like it or not, we are different, we are holy, we are called to stand in judgment on wickedness—our own included. We don't need to be self-righteous when we judge the sin of others, if in genuine sadness we condemn our own. And it isn't hypocrisy to reach for more than we can currently grasp. It isn't hypocrisy to pursue a purer, braver, more honorable lifestyle than we now possess, if we do it in the name of the Christ!

It isn't hard to understand that we don't want people to see us as smug and superior. (We've seen people we thought were like that, and it made us sick.) But the answer to the fear of coming across like that isn't in denying who—and whose—we are. The answer isn't to be found in watering down what we have been called to. We can't join others in their sin or grin about their wickedness, nor should we "understand" immorality too well. Our eye is not to be on people and what they think about us so much as it is to be on God and what he thinks about us.

It could be that the world doesn't mind our standing up for what is true and clean and just and kind. Maybe we worry too much about that. Maybe they spend more time behind our backs, shaking their heads in disappointment at our lack of forthrightness. Maybe they'd dearly love to see a community of believers cheerfully and bravely taking a stand.

Yes, I know there are believers who act like butter wouldn't melt in their mouths. I know there are people who give the impression they have no sin to repent of, that they and sin are perfect strangers, while all the while they're tirelessly (and with relish) damning the world to hell. This is deplorable, and I seem to recall Jesus speaking a parable about two men who went up to the temple to pray. One was overwhelmed by his sinfulness and the other was overwhelmed by his own moral magnificence (he was one of those, said the text, "who trusted in themselves that they were righteous").[1]

Just the same, I seem to see and hear more about our *lack* of difference ("we're no better than anyone else") than our being too "saintly." The desire not to appear different, not to sound different, is being swallowed up in the desire to be "humble" and "unassuming." We want to protect our own reputation before our peers, so we let God's reputation go to the wall. It's all perfectly understandable, but it's all out of line with who we are and what we've been called to. We can't do this. This must disappoint God terribly.

> **We want to protect our own reputation before our peers, so we let God's reputation go to the wall.**

No motive, however noble it appears, is a good one if it results in our keeping the light of God from people in darkness. Insisting that we are 'saints' might raise a smile or two even if we do it in the best possible spirit, but we weren't called by God to be put off by a sneer or a belly laugh. I can think of specific occasions in my life when, had I been more forthright in my profession of holiness, I could have avoided temptation as well as borne witness to the living Christ.

When the Roman troops first came to the shores of Britain, the hardy old Brit warriors, looking down at them from the cliff tops, might not have been too impressed. But the first thing they saw those troops do was assemble in formation on the beach to watch their ships being burned. Whatever else these soldiers down below had in mind, they weren't planning to leave; they'd come to stay. They were committed, and there was no turning back. Burning their boats would rib their purpose with strength.

Something like that happens when Christians, without undue noise, make it clear they have committed to Christ. They create an air of expectation that is not only good for those who experience it, but good for themselves. To burn our boats in the presence of our "enemies" makes it harder for us to turn back. And there are desperate people outside of Christ, drowning in evil and despair at its strength, who need brave models to give them hope.

No, we shouldn't hide the fact that we are saints.

# The Adventure of Holiness

✦

The weapons we fight with are not the weapons
of the world. On the contrary, they have divine
power to demolish strongholds. We demolish
arguments and every pretention that sets itself
up against the knowledge of God, and we
take captive every thought to make it
obedient to Christ.
—2 Corinthians 10:4–5

Holiness isn't dullness. It isn't to be associated with lines of pale-faced, gaunt, passionless men and women who chant in Latin as they make their way to cold and dreary cells to end their day in prayer. And it isn't to be equated with "quiet times" when the lonely soul wrestles with its God in prayer or meditates on ways it can be more free from the chains that bind it.

I'm far from thinking that retreat from the hustle and bustle of life is always a bad thing. I'm sure we've all learned something of the importance of being alone with God. But I can't help thinking that holiness, like self-denial, has been too long associated with negation, withdrawal, retreat, blandness, and irrelevance. We associate it more with what we *should not* do or say or think than with what we *should*. Even when we see it in a more positive light, we seem to see it mainly in terms of a slog through mud and clinging grime. And of course, in some respects, it is that. But that's only part of the story.

Too often we make it appear that sin is alive with color and holiness is pale gray. Sin is romantic; holiness is passionless. Sin is life loving; holiness is life denying. Sin cheerfully goes in search of more; holiness gloomily hangs on to less. But shouldn't we be speaking of holiness in brighter, more glorious, and living terms? Isn't it true that holiness is the more noble quest? And if it is, why shouldn't we describe it in terms to match its nature?

Sin is not romantic—no matter how many violins are playing in the background. It is not full of life and openhearted. It isn't heroic! It's a gutless surrender to the darkness within us, an unpardonable laying down of our weapons in a war from which we mustn't withdraw.

Holiness is a bold protest against the moral flatness of the course of this world. It is a refusal to live like the herd, a refusal to run like Gadarene pigs down the slope to destruction. It is nailing God's colors to the masts of our lives; it is running up the flag of the crucified and living One at the citadel of our souls. It's saying no to the easy compromise, the seductive slime, the sewer of selfishness, the greedy business policies, the limitless expanding of corporate power, the insatiable sexual appetite, the smug self-righteousness, the hypocrisy of racism and other forms of elitism.

An earnest pursuit of holiness is more demanding than an Everest climb, more exciting than a battle with the Colorado River on a raft, more exhilarating than skydiving, more important than winning the Pulitzer or the Nobel Peace Prize. There's nothing dull about it! Destinies are at stake, a world hangs in the balance as the covenanted community of God's people fervently, but without fever, hacks its way through a world overgrown with noxious weeds, fed by scum-covered swamps, bringing a gospel of health and healing to the people of the world.

Of course, sections of a sophisticated Western society choke with laughter at such talk, but that is only another mark of their blindness and their dire need. And, yes, even some Christians think that all this is just so much melodrama. ("Let's not get carried away.") That's only another proof that the people of God are needed in this world. A plague sweeps the planet, digesting as it advances. Some of the people of God fall victim to it and are swallowed up in the sucking, suffocating mire—but this is even more reason for the rest to march, bravely and cleanly, on their way through the world, healing and rescuing as they go, doing the will of their holy Master who never leaves their side.

We see nothing more exciting anywhere in the world than men and women taking on the Word Hater for the glory of their Lord and the saving of fellow-humans. Watch their costly and difficult transformation as they fight entrenched evil and malignant foes, often under extraordinarily difficult circumstances, taking enemy strongholds for their Lord and Master. See them work together, nurturing one another, forgiving and protecting one another, dragging each other to safety, closing ranks around those under special danger and placing themselves under threat in their efforts to keep wounded soldiers from dying.

Say we don't want a life like that; say it makes too many demands and shows too little success for the effort; say we'd rather just drift with the currents and follow the crowd; say we prefer the easy pleasures over the hand-to-hand combat—which in some areas, never seems to end. Say anything, but don't say it's dull!

That's not only to reject the call of God on us; it's pathetically stupid!

# Negotiations and Referendums

✦

But who are you, O man, to talk back to God?

"Shall what is formed say to him who formed it,

'Why did you make me like this?'"

—Romans 9:20

The apostle Peter says, "It is better, if it is God's will, to suffer for doing good than for doing evil."[1] "So then, those who suffer according to God's will should commit themselves to their faithful Creator and continue to do good."[2]

Let's get some things clear about the will of God as it relates to the "resident aliens" to whom Peter writes. Peter's readers were God's elect; they were ransomed by the sacrifice of his Son; they had heard the Good News and made him Lord of their lives. In making him Lord, they placed themselves under his will and determined not only to obey that will, but to grow so they would *will* that will, so his will would become theirs.

With that in mind, these people didn't enter into negotiations with God on how he would or would not structure their lives. They didn't enter a debating session with the sovereign Lord; rather, they became his devoted servants who dedicated themselves to furthering his purposes and not their own. Having acknowledged his lordship over them (they didn't confer it on him), they weren't offered the option of calling a personal referendum every time he willed something that might not bring them pleasure.

But, though the God they received as Lord was absolute sovereign in their lives, he is no tyrant. His purpose is not to abuse or destroy. This he demonstrated, and this they joyfully acknowledged, in the person of Jesus Christ. What this God would will, however complex or painful, could have no other purpose but his own glory shown in their eternal blessedness.

In light of this, if he willed suffering for them, it was not for them to debate it; though of course, in their pain they might well have debated it. But in their better moments, they would still say, "Not my will, but thine be done."

> Having acknowledged his lordship over them, they weren't offered the option of calling a personal referendum every time he willed something that might not bring them pleasure.

In the days of the Scottish Covenanters, when Alan Cameron, the father of Richard, was lying in prison, they brought the head and hands of his son to him ("to add grief to his sorrow") and asked him if he recognized them. "I know them! I know them," said the old man as he bent over to kiss them. Then while praising and weeping he said, "It is the Lord! Good is the will of the Lord."[3]

But could God will suffering? Yes! Peter goes on to speak of impenitent rebels who flung God's patience back in his face. For years he pleaded with them through Noah to turn from their wickedness, but they spurned his grace and suffered the consequences.[4]

But could God will suffering for people who were gladly obedient to him? Yes! He willed it for his own Son, Jesus Christ.

The Scots preacher Arthur Gossip wrote,

> Had I been in Jerusalem during those hours in which Christ was betrayed, and tried, and retried, and condemned, and mocked, and led to Calvary, I would have prayed—ah! how I would have prayed, and with that passionate insistence—that God would burst in, must burst in before it was too late, "for Christ's sake," and for his kingdom's sake, and for the sake of the poor, desperate, unsaved world, but always, always for Christ's sake, that he be not shamed, and His glorious enterprise fizzle out in mockery. Yet, had that confident prayer of mine—offered, mark you, "for Christ's sake"—been heard and granted, where would that same poor, desperate world have been today?[5]

In a world that rejects God, those who are God's risk rejection also. In a world that rejects Jesus, those who are identified with Jesus risk rejection also. They came to God in Christ, knowing how Father and Son were treated by the world; so why should they think it strange if they should be treated in the same way?[6]

There is a suffering that only God's people can know! In a world like ours, those who identify themselves with the God of Jesus Christ identify themselves with a God who is bent on the rescue of the world. They need to make up their minds to that—as Jesus did!

Didn't he say, "The Son of man must suffer many things"?[7] And when speaking to the two on the Emmaus road, didn't he press them with, "Did not the Christ have to suffer these things?"[8] There's that "must," that "have to." And in Gethsemane, didn't he say he would rather not drink, but followed that with a "nevertheless" and drank?

Satan said to him in the wilderness, "If you're the Son of God, you ought to enjoy yourself. You shouldn't lack bread; you shouldn't have to wrestle with fears; you ought to be lord of the kingdoms; you ought to live like a billionaire, walk where you will, and reign like a sovereign. If you really are the Son of God, you would be his 'pet' and wouldn't have to go through all this wilderness hardship."[9]

Christ's devastating response was to reverse all that. Precisely because he was the Son of God (a God who was possessed with a loving longing to bless and rescue), he must feel the hunger, fears, longings, burdens, and oppression of the people of the world. There is no redemption at a distance!

Of the Master, George Matheson—who wrote the beautiful hymn, "O Love That Will Not Let Me Go"— said,

Had He been less good He would have been less burdened. His purity made His pain; His tenderness made His tears; His selflessness made His sorrow; His righteousness made Him restless; His luster made Him lonely; His kindness made Him kinless; His crown made His cross. It was because He was the Son of Man He had nowhere to lay His head.[10]

And to the servants, Peter said, "It is better if it is God's will, to suffer for doing good . . . because Christ died for sins . . . the righteous for the unrighteous, to bring you to God."[11]

"But wait," their peers would have said, "if you were the people of God, you shouldn't be going through hard times. A God worth anything would not allow his people to endure hardship." And the Christians would have answered: "You're wrong. It is precisely because we are the people of God that we are burdened. And it's precisely because he is a God worth having and seeks to save you that he wills suffering for us, on your behalf."

God willed the suffering of Christ to bring them to God. And if that same God willed suffering for Christ's followers, that he might bring others to himself, what would be strange about that? What kind of God did we think we were getting involved with?

Ah, yes, but that would mean our suffering was the result of the choice of sinners doing what God hated. Yes! And so? It is no less the will of God. He chooses that we endure the contradiction of sinners and bear the cursing of unbelievers. He could put a stop to it but won't. More than that, he chooses not to put a stop to it and to use their hateful ways to bring them an offer of redemption—even though it's at our expense.

Does this offend us? Did it offend us that he did it for us in Christ? God sent Christ into the world, and Christ prayed that we be left in the world[12]—for the world's sake! We not only share the human troubles of a fallen humanity, we may be called to suffer at their hands!

Of course the Cross of Christ was there because the religious leaders feared political repercussions if he wasn't killed. Of course the Cross was there because Pilate was weak and fearful, because witnesses could be paid to lie, because Judas loved money, because the multitudes wouldn't speak up for him. Of course all this is true. The Cross was the will of sinful people. But it was the will of *God* through sinful people.

Perhaps the real question is not, Might God will suffering for us at the hands of evil people? but, Are we willing that he should do so?

# Dead Heave

◆

I run in the path of your commands,

for you have set my heart free.

—Psalm 119:32

Those of us inclined to worry or to be oversensitive can hardly help but feel uneasy when they hear a strong call to holiness. It isn't that we don't want to be holy or are reluctant to engage in the pursuit of holiness; it's simply that we're afraid, not yet fully persuaded that God will not cast us out if our efforts don't appear to be very successful. (We even worry about that worry.)

Some of Christ's friends, with their upright lives and their hard speech, deepen our worries. If God is like them, we feel we're in real trouble. God's love for us has not been perfected in us; our fears may have their hiding places, but they still hang around.[1]

We long to imitate Christ, to reflect his glory and purity, his gallantry and selflessness, but we find it a daunting task. And every call to be like Christ is at the same time a spike that gouges us.

Leslie D. Weatherhead, noted World War II British preacher, went to hear the famous Austrian violinist Fritz Kreisler. He confessed that within minutes he was emotionally overcome by the beauty and power of the performance.

"Tell me to imitate him?" asks Weatherhead. "How *can* I?" I can imitate the way he wears his hair. I can imitate his tie and his baggy trousers. But if I tried for a thousand years I could never play like that. . . . Nothing could take me where he is. He has received a gift."[2]

Yes, that's the problem for many of us. The glory of the Christ makes a constant demand of us, and we haven't learned to follow the call without being discouraged by our dreadful lack of progress. And if we aren't careful, in despair we'll falter completely. If Christ's friends aren't careful, their accurate but cold condemnation of us will add to our sense of despair.

So life can become a dead heave rather than a gift to be enjoyed.

Holiness can become a gloomy threat rather than a joyous and liberating pursuit, with a constant eye to actual and possible failures.

That's what the Scottish theologian H.R. Mackintosh was talking about when he said:

> Is there not too much "forced labour" in religion? How many Christians never get beyond a

feeling of painful compulsion in that region of life! They serve God because they must, and because, if they do not, or try to run away, the most dreadful consequences may follow. No one observing them would ever be reminded of that Bible phrase which speaks of "joy and peace in believing."

Take for example the man who is toiling at the culture or reformation of character, and is finding the whole business miserably disappointing. He does his best to keep right with his conscience, and a very brave fight, often, he makes of it. He watches himself as a nurse might watch a patient, not to say a detective watch a criminal. When he fails, it only makes him stricter with himself; more rules are drawn up; he cuts out this indulgence and that other; there are new precautions and refinements of self-control. But the whole thing is a dead heave, day after day. Conscience may keep him to the laborious task, but his heart is not in it. It is not a happy kind of religion, and certainly it is not infectious.[3]

The difficulty of the task gives no one the right to give up on it. The grace and gifts of God offer no one exemption from the desire and pursuit of holiness as it is seen in Christ. The unbridgeable gap between the holiness of God in Christ and our own (all of us!) meager character is no excuse for not cherishing the ideal as we see it in Jesus.

**The difficulty of the task gives no one the right to give up on it.**

But it doesn't help us to gain that depth of soul we all (all of us!) long for, if we think God has left us to our own unaided possibilities or is tracking us with a stopwatch. It doesn't help us to gain holiness if we're always severely beaten for failures, if we're always reminded of past wrongs, if we're not given the assurance that he who began a good work in us will himself complete it in the day of our Lord.

But he will complete it, for "he who called us is faithful"![4]

♦

# SEVEN

# VISION

I have always felt that there
was a compliment to the
human race, and a fine
appeal to all that is best in
man, in the Christian doctrine
of the Fall. It seems to me a
horrid thing to suggest that
man as he is is just about
right. It is surely a far kinder
thing to say . . . it is nearer
the truth to say that man as
he is is all wrong.

—John A. Hutton

✦

# What the Cynic Saw

✦

Blessed are the pure in heart,

for they will see God.

—Matthew 5:8

American preacher and author Clarence McCartney said, "The sun shines down on nothing more wonderful than a lovely human being."[1] Nature provides some lovely sights—autumn forests ablaze with color, majestic mountain ranges, stupendous canyons that make you dizzy with wonder, frothy white waterfalls falling hundreds of feet down cliff faces, raging oceans teeming with gentle giants and gliding creatures, tropical islands dotted with green-blue lagoons, bronze fields of grain swaying in the breeze, and vast herds of animals full of grace and power. All soul-stirring. No wonder poets and dreamers spend time on them.

But not one of them even begins to compare with a man, woman, girl, or boy of high moral character and generosity of spirit.

The God who took Job on a tour of the creation was no stranger to all the wonders he'd made, but it was a human he singled out to stake his own reputation on.[2] "Have you considered my servant Job? There is no one like him on the earth, a blameless and upright man who fears God and turns away from evil."[3] (Why must some writers attribute pettiness to God in these places? Why must they suggest that he is mischievously needling Satan? Why not allow it to stand as it stands? Why can't even God find the sight of a beautiful person something to exult in? Why not?)

God and Satan both looked at the same thing: one saw purity and the other saw hypocrisy; one saw devotion and the other saw self-serving; one saw glory and the other saw grime. God, the wise and holy lover, saw the man as glorious.

But God has a history of seeing things like this. In Jesus Christ he walked up to a hated collaborator called Matthew, eyed him as he sat there fleecing his own people in the name of the occupational forces. "Leave all that and follow me," he said. He said it as if he expected him to do it, and astonishingly, Matthew did it![4] It was there all the time and nobody saw it in the man but God. Jaundiced and bitter eyes saw a heartless, self-serving loser who injured his own, but God saw him as an apostle to the world who would die poor, spreading the precious word of salvation.

The same is true with how God looks at his people. The fearful Balak hired Balaam to curse Israel because he could only see her as fit to be damned. But God, looking down on his sinful people camped in the valley of Moab, said through the hireling, "How beautiful are your tents, O Jacob."[5]

It's only a half truth (though a nice half) to say that love is blind. T. E. Jessop, in his book *Law and Love*, reminds us that love is considerate, but, he says,

> What is considerateness but a careful consider-ing or thinking about how the interests of the persons loved are to be maintained or furthered? Some folks never do think hard until they are in love, and it is under the stimulus of love that thinking often does its best. When love demands it, quite ordinary people can rise to unaccus-tomed effort on the plane of thought.[6]

The best kind of thinking, the best kind of appraisal, is that which is moved by love of the person; the best kind of appraisal is that which lovingly considers what must be done to bless and enrich the person.

Cynicism and cold criticism don't have the tools or the capacity to see well, and that, ultimately, is the difference between how God saw Job and how Satan saw him. Of course, Job had failures; but the trouble with Satan and those who relish grim truths is that they act as though these ugly truths are the whole story. But chapters 29 and 31 of the book of Job paint such a lovely picture of the man. Satan couldn't bear to take that kind of truth at face value or allow it to carry weight.

The eager critic has the same problem. The grim truths he knows must be made the essence of his victim's life, don't you see. Everything fine and good and true must be ignored or played down, and the grim truths (real or perceived) must be kept forefront in the critic's mind and heart. (As I write these words I feel the conviction of sin in this particular area so sharply that it's like a heavy blow to my chest.)

Offended righteousness becomes blind in the twinkling of an eye. Mercy is hemmed in behind a high wall of justice. A justice cold enough to freeze salt water; a justice that can't make allowances, or worse—doesn't know how to make allowances. The most miserable character in all of Victor Hugo's massive *Les Miserables* (the miserable ones) is Javert, the worshiper of justice. Javert was a policeman who committed suicide because he couldn't bear the fact that he had shown mercy to a guilty person.

One of the tragic things about tireless criticism is that it always has something to feed on. There is enough dishonor around to keep the critical spirit busy without having to invent things or tell lies—there is plenty to "justify" spiteful criticism. So those of us whose dishonor is of the "scarlet" and public kind are grist for the critic's mill. Why would we think otherwise? Didn't even the noncynical Nathan assure David his behavior had been the grounds for reproach against God?

**As I write these words I feel the conviction of sin so sharply that it's like a heavy blow to my chest.**

At this moment I realize, at a level deeper than intellect, the truth of what I'm saying, for I have sinned greatly in this area, as in others.

For Satan to be as relentless as he is against Job, he must ignore the vast depths of kindness, decency, integrity, compassion, generosity, and goodness within his victim. And for any of us to be carried away by some truths we know (or think we know) so that our victim's life is shriveled down to the size of those truths, so that our victim has no richness of life beyond those truths— for us to do that, we must ignore all that speaks on his or her behalf. We must shut our ears to all the true and lovely things spoken of him. We must close our eyes to all the goodness we see displayed. We must close our hearts to all the noble work that God is doing in and through him. Because if we allow other lovely truths to have their full voice about this person, we may not be able to continue our role as the relentless critic.

If only we could see like God. We can, of course, can't we? But it requires being like God, doesn't it?

# Smoking and Smugness

✦

To some who were confident of their own
righteousness and looked down on
everybody else, Jesus told this parable.
—Luke 18:9

We went to Furr's cafeteria. There were about eight
or nine of us, all dedicated preachers of Christ.
We were going to discuss better ways and means to reach
the unforgiven on earth with the saving message of Jesus
Christ.

Since none of us smoke we found seats in the section
marked: Nonsmoking Section. Not long after we began
our fervent discussion about saving the unforgiven, three
ladies sat down at the table next to ours. At least one of
them lit up a cigarette and contentedly puffed away.

241

The smoke and the smell reached our dedicated little group. Up went the heads, sniff went the noses, and then the muttering began. The murmur increased to a low-key protest—the nerve of that woman who was infringing on our rights! We had our rights! we told one another.

I was closest to her. And above the rising din of protesting and indignant men, the lady caught my words. I don't remember what they were—some remark about people taking other people's rights away by smoking in a clearly marked nonsmoking area. She turned to me immediately and humbly apologized. "I'm very sorry. I didn't know this was a nonsmoking section." She extinguished her cigarette and returned to visiting with her friends.

I was too embarrassed by her genuine apology to say anything in return. I should have resisted that and apologized to *her*. She had acted in a Christian manner.

Instead of our muttering against the lady, we should have gently asked her if she was aware that she was in a nonsmoking section. That is, if we had felt the need of insisting on our rights at all. I don't remember much of what was said in the next hour. I was thinking of the reason for our gathering. I was wondering what chance the unforgiven on earth had if those who went preaching went as we were. As I was.

I'm still amazed, at times, at my smugness and at the utter inconsistency and incompatibility between the attitude I showed there and my stated desire. Whatever would happen to the rest of the earth, there was a lady right there next to us who didn't even receive as much as a kind word from one of us. It amazes me yet that I was virtually saying to that woman that she would have to act to suit me if she expected me to reflect Christ before her.

I'm amazed that we were planning to send young men and women out into all the earth to adjust, submit, give up rights, say good-bye to comforts and pleasures in order to manifest Christ verbally and vitally, while we couldn't endure a lady encroaching on our space.

God, help us. God, forgive us! God, deliver us from delivering implicit ultimatums such as: Make yourself acceptable to me, and I'll share Christ with you. God, give us a clearer vision of ourselves and redeem us from becoming or remaining pompous asses.

*Smoking*

*and*

*Smugness*

♦

# Formulas and Experience

✦

Having a form of godliness but denying its power.

Have nothing to do with them.

—2 Timothy 3:5

My favorite story about Mrs. Einstein is when reporters were asking her if she understood Albert's big words. She said she understood a lot of them, one at a time; it was when he put them together in sentences that things got tough. Then they asked her if she understood his two theories of relativity. She said, "No . . . but you can trust Albert!"

Don't you love that? She couldn't understand the jargon or the deeper doctrines, but she knew the man. The formulas and equations had her beat, but on the relational kind of truths she was the world's leading authority on her husband.

It's perfectly legitimate (and unavoidable) to describe life and living realities in words and phrases (as far as that is possible), but often those who define them best understand them least and those who define them most poorly know them best! This is verified when you meet up with people who profess no religious faith but whose lives are noble and gallant—as distinct from those who can recite, word-perfect, their religious creed or reams of Scripture but whose lives are narrow, joyless, trivial, or self-righteous (or any combination of these).

There's a mental disorder (I've forgotten its Latin name) that affects the poor victim like this. He pores over maps, memorizes places, rivers, roads, points of departure and points of arrival, mountains and valleys and the like. And then, in his confusion, he thinks he has made the trip. A specialist in the religious manifestation of this disorder describes it like this: "The peril of religion is that vital experience shall be resolved into a formula of explanation, and that men, grasping the formula, shall suppose themselves thereby to possess the experience."

Howard Butt tells us in *The Velvet Covered Brick* that back in 1950 some young people discovered a gold mine in New York.[1] It was during the peak months when *South Pacific* was playing on Broadway. Rodgers and Hammerstein's blockbuster was enjoying sellout crowds as the European heartthrob, Ezio Pinza, sang to America's sweetheart, Mary Martin. People came from every little town in the country to see the show, but they hadn't a hope. Tickets were nonexistent. The young New Yorkers picked up or bought used ticket stubs or programs around the theater and sold them to rural Americans who didn't want to go home confessing they hadn't seen the show. Back home in the sticks, with programs and ticket stubs in hand and humming a few well-rehearsed bars of "Some Enchanted Evening" the big-timers made their friends jealous. They had everything—everything but the experience!

Secondhand religion is a poor substitute for the real thing. But, then, so is secondhand living. To allow society to pour you into its own mold is as bad for non-Christians as it is for Christians. A few beers, a couple of weeks in Spain each year, hours of television each day, and a "lie in" on Sunday morning is hardly living. A dusty Bible, church attendance a couple of times a week, and copious tears over the documentary that shows the exploitation and rape of millions isn't much better.

It's as sad a spectacle to see religious people with their hearsay religion berate the "unbelievers" as it is to see unbelievers with their borrowed philosophy, tired old arguments against God's existence, and anti-church feelings berate the churchgoers. While they're hammering each other, life is slipping by and noble causes with eternal consequences are left unsupported by both camps.

Speaking as one Christian, I believe we're all going to meet God, and if we're living on "formulas," we're going to answer for not having some genuine experience of life.

# The Rewards of Integrity

✦

Keeping a clear conscience, so that those who
speak maliciously against your good behavior in
Christ may be ashamed of their slander.

—1 Peter 3:16

The Bible tells the story of Jacob. As a younger man
he had taken advantage of his twin brother and
extorted from him the major share of the family inheritance. A little while later he fooled his aged father,
cheated the brother out of further blessing, and then fled
the country. Now, twenty years later, he must return to
face his twin, which has him scared witless. Had Jacob
been upright, he wouldn't have been worried sick.

Shakespeare was right: "Conscience doth make cowards
of us all." Our mouths go dry, our pulse hammers in our

throat at the mere thought of our shame being discovered. We imagine people are talking about us, snubbing us, avoiding us. A letter not answered or a phone call not returned torments us with the thought that our "secret" is known. The pain we endure as a result of our lack of honor so far outweighs any pleasure dishonor brings that it's a wonder any of us stoops to being treacherous.

Somewhere I read of a young man who tried to talk a young lady into sexual intercourse, but she wouldn't hear of it. Then he offered her booze she wouldn't touch. A little later he wanted to share some drugs with her, but she turned those down too. By this time he was thoroughly disgusted and sulky (should have been thoroughly ashamed) and demanded to know what she did for fun. Hmmm, what was it she said? Something like:

> I never have to worry about being diseased or pregnant. That means I don't have to wrestle with a decision to abort an unwanted baby. And that's fun! And I don't have to wonder if I'm being pawed over by someone who might not want to know me a couple of months from now. I never have any difficulty remembering what I did the night before and who I did it with; and, listen, that's fun. I'm looking forward to the day when I can give myself totally to my husband rather than a worn-down piece of me to an acquaintance in the backseat of some car. And that's fun. I won't ever have to worry about getting a blood test that tells me I'm HIV positive or have some venereal disease; and believe me, that's fun. Even though my parents love me so much that they would stand by me if I ever got into trouble, I never have to worry about seeing

them crushed and shamed by some disgraceful behavior of mine—and that's really fun!

I reflect on that, and I'm tempted to think it sounds old-fashioned—light-years away from where we are in society today. But, you know, that isn't true. There are kids by the millions throughout the world who think that way and behave that way.

It's just that the "bad news" shouts louder than the good. But the good news is that the bad news, while it really is bad, is not as bad as we're being told. And even if it were, isn't there something grand about the girl's clean, strong approach to things?

Evelyn, a teenage friend of Norman Vincent Peale, was under pressure in school from some "broad-minded" friends to "go all the way." She told her father they made it all sound so natural, that now and then she wondered what she was waiting for. He said: "I think I can tell you—you're waiting to be free! Free from the nagging voice of conscience, from the uneasiness. Free to give all of yourself, not a panicky fraction. Something in you, some deep instinct keeps telling you not to blur it, not to waste or cheapen it." Then he added, "Tell your broad-minded friends not to be so broad-minded that their brains fall out."[1]

Don't you love that?

> The pain we endure as a result of our lack of honor so far outweighs any pleasure dishonor brings that it's a wonder any of us stoops to being treacherous.

When he was a teenager, the famous preacher Harry E. Fosdick wrote a letter to the girl he was going to marry.

> I know you are alive out there somewhere, thinking of and looking for me as I'm looking for you. One day we'll meet, we'll fall in love and be married. And because I believe that you're keeping yourself for me, so that you can love me in a way that you will love no one else in all the world, I'll maintain my integrity too and keep myself for you.[2]

And he did. Years later, he said that his making and keeping a profound covenant with a girl he hadn't even met gave him purpose and more satisfaction than he ever dreamed possible.

One of the rewards of integrity is that it brings to those glorious people a deep sense of profound joy and satisfaction. But centrally, for those who have given themselves to Christ before they've given themselves to anyone else, integrity pleases him for whom all glorious deeds are done.

I've taken a beating when I was innocent, and I've taken a beating when I was guilty, and I can tell you, there's no fun in being beaten when you've asked for it. At least when you're innocent in the matter, you can always go away from the beating with the inner comfort that this time, if the truth were known, you suffered unjustly. And that, even in the midst of pain, is fun!

# Gyp

✦

Brothers, I do not consider myself yet to have
taken hold of it. But one thing I do:
Forgetting what is behind and
straining toward what is ahead.
—Philippians 3:13

Pericles was one of ancient Greece's greatest orators
as well as one of its greatest statesman. I've read that
he refused to speak more than two or three times a year
in the senate, even though he attended regularly and even
though everyone entreated him to speak when he was
there. He thought that making too many speeches hurt
a man and hurt his hearers and hurt the noble causes
they all espoused. So he didn't speak very often, and as a
consequence, when he did, it had a real impact. The

principles involved here apply to more than making speeches or preaching sermons.

Author Frank Boreham told about John Broadbank, a man who hadn't learned to say no. He got involved in every project he came across and spoke at every conference he was invited to. The more he traveled, the greater his fame grew, and the greater the fame, the more he was invited to various boards and conference platforms. His family suffered loss in all this, and one day his devoted wife sobbed out to him how lonely she was and how guilty she felt for feeling that way. A week at home without a project made him realize how much of a whirl his life had become. It was about that time that he came across Gyp.

Broadbank was walking across a field when he saw a man down by a pond drowning a terrier dog. Broadbank asked him why and the man said: "Well, you see, sir, when he was a pup he was all right and we were fond of him. We call him Gypsy—Gyp for short. But now he's gotten to be a regular nuisance. We're always losing him. He follows everybody and the dog that follows everybody is no good to anybody." Broadbank pleaded with the man to give him the dog, which he did. John walked off with the terrier. "Come on Gyp," he said, "I've been a bit of a gypsy myself. You and I will teach each other better manners."[1]

But it's more than a question of better manners, isn't it! It becomes a question of fruitfulness, and sometimes, a question of character. It may be tempting to believe your own press and think that the world of speeches, sermons, noble causes, and community projects would be utterly impoverished without you (if they could survive at all). But it's a mistake to spread yourself too thin. As John

Broadbank finally admitted: "On the whole, it's better to be narrow and deep."

I was amazed (and pleased) to read a few years ago Billy Graham quoted as saying that if he had it all to do again he would "speak less and study more." Imagine that, coming from a man who has probably addressed more people than any other religious man in history.

Teaching, like character—if it's to be rich and fruitful—has to put down deep roots. In the end, "nibbling on the run" destroys the effectiveness and fruitfulness of a teacher or speaker. It robs others too. The speeches begin to bristle with clichés, one-liners, and well-worn stories that grow more wonderful with the telling. People are no longer impressed with the "flair" and sorely hunger for something substantial (or at least sorely needing it even if they don't hunger for it). They begin to realize, as J. S. Stewart put it, that "the Lord was not in the wind." Wouldn't it be sad if Christ, asked where I was, said: "I can't say, I keep losing him. He follows everybody."

◆

# Things I Didn't Do

✦

If anyone gives even a cup of cold water to one

of these little ones because he is my disciple,

I tell you the truth,

he will certainly not lose his reward.

—Matthew 10:42

D o I need to tell any of you how distressed I am at times over lost opportunities to do good, express love, or speak a word for Christ? Haven't you experienced the same thing? My intention to be kind and caring to people (tomorrow) goes on the assumption that those I wish to reach will be around tomorrow!

Once when my mother wasn't feeling very well, I went by to see her. The house was tiny, the stairs to the little bedroom were steep, and her bed, while not large, seemed huge as she lay there (she wasn't five feet tall). We talked a while, and as I was leaving, I stood behind the bedroom door and worked up the nerve to tell her I loved her. (Don't ask me why it was difficult—I don't know. I have always blamed it on one thing or another.)

She didn't respond, so I glanced around the door and saw her quietly weeping. If I'd only known! The last time I saw my little mother, she was crying at our door as my family and I left the country for a while. I told her it wouldn't be long until I was back, but she died before I had the chance to fulfill my intention to "really" show her what love is.

No, it isn't true. I did see her one more time—when I came back for the funeral. I whispered to her and kissed her, but there was no response. I had blundered terribly.

Friends have moved away and I've lost track of them over the years. How I wish, I tell myself, I had been more of a friend when the opportunity was there. I have determined to do what I know to do (as much as I am able) and to do the things I'm stirred to do, promptly!

Some sad and remorseful girl wrote this poem, which has haunted me since I read it. It's called: "Things You Didn't Do."

> Remember the day I borrowed your brand new car and I dented it?
> I thought you'd kill me, but you didn't.
> And remember the day I dragged you to the beach, and you said it would rain, and it did?
> I thought you'd say, "I told you so!" But you didn't.
> Do you remember the time I flirted with all the guys to make you jealous, and you were?

I thought you'd leave me, but you didn't.
Do you remember the time I spilt strawberry pie
      all over your car rug?
I thought you'd hit me, but you didn't.
And remember the time I forgot to tell you the
      dance was formal and you showed up in
      jeans?
I thought you'd drop me, but you didn't.
Yes, there were lots of things you didn't do.
But you put up with me, and you loved me,
  and you protected me.
There were lots of things I wanted to make up to
      you when you returned from Viet Nam.
But you didn't.[1]

*Things*

*I Didn't*

*Do*

♦

259

I want to love and serve and cherish and confront and comfort and inspire *now!* I don't want to develop the habit of putting off the good that I know and feel like doing. And I will not let my failures to fulfill this purpose overwhelm me. I've made up my mind, and by the grace of God I'll see it through. I know I won't be perfect in anything. But I will improve! I will exercise myself unto service, moment by moment, opportunity by opportunity. I will not wait until the "significant" occasion arises.

I know if I am faithful in little that the much will take care of itself under God's hand. From this moment on I will have fewer bitter memories of things I didn't do and more joy in the realization that I've been a channel of blessing to some people in little but significant ways by doing it now.

# A Badge of Honor

✦

For it has been granted to you on behalf of

Christ not only to believe on him,

but also to suffer for him.

—Philippians 1:29

Over and over again Job begged God to ease his pain, to remove his heavy hand from him that he might have peace. In Job's case, though he didn't know it, the pain existed because of his integrity. The pain was inflicted on Job's behalf.

You're well aware that the man had been slandered by Satan and that God had gone to Job's defense by taking away the wages by which Satan had said Job was bought and paid for. Job's ignorance made the suffering more acute and the mental torment all the more cutting.

His ignorance only made his bravery more brave, but had he known the reasons for the suffering, he would gladly have endured it all. He would have been fully aware of the incredible honor God was bestowing on him by making him humanity's champion against the dark forces of evil and cynicism. Had he known what was happening, he would almost certainly not have asked for the pain to be removed—it was a badge of his honor, don't you see. Still, the pain was real, the suffering was prolonged and acute, the agony would still bring groans and longings for ease.

Something similar has happened to great sufferers down through the years, even to the present day. Without being glib and without suggesting that words automatically banish the grinding effects of prolonged suffering, it's still true that gallant sufferers embrace their pain and sometimes find joy in and through it. Let me illustrate this with an actual case involving dear friends of mine.

They had been married for more than fifteen years. She was devoted to God, her husband, and their children; she worked long hours without complaint for years to support him through his demanding studies. Shortly after successfully completing his education, the husband walked away from the marriage and claimed he was making a brave bid for freedom. She was beside herself with grief—complex grief, involving her faith, her children, and the man she adored. So when I met her at the airport to talk about it, she was fragmented and sobbing much of the time. She missed him in Christ and was mainly concerned about his relationship with God which, in his "brave bid for freedom," was jettisoned. While she wanted him back, wanted the family united (and she made no bones about that), she wanted to see him back with Christ above everything else.

And how was she holding up? I asked. She was having no faith crisis, but she was finding the pain almost unbearable. She had asked God to take away the pain, and she knew, she said, "If I could really give the matter over to God, my pain would cease." This was playing havoc with her inner world.

Some well-intentioned friends assured her that God was eager to remove her pain. The agony would vanish, they told her, if she would simply "give it over to God." In fact, then, her continuing pain was the result of her flawed response to the tragedy. God wanted to remove it immediately, but she was hindering him, they told her.

Nobody knows enough to talk this way.

And why did she think the pain existed in the first place? I asked her. She said she couldn't stop loving the man and grieving over the disruption of the family. That made perfect sense. So was she supposed to forget all the lovely years they had had together, the warmth, the intimacy, the smiles, the victories shared, the losses overcome together, the companionship? Was she to obliterate all the memories created, all her feelings, the hopes and dreams generated and worked for? When she asked God to remove the pain, did she want him to do a lobotomy on her? to make her someone other than she was? If she cared nothing for the man, if she could dismiss more than fifteen covenant years as though they hadn't existed, she wouldn't be the person she was!

Bad enough that the pain was ploughing deep into her soul, worse that she should think its very existence indicted her for her lack of piety. She was too trusting to suggest that God was unwilling to remove it; she attributed its continued existence to herself (which is part of the truth).

Why not view her suffering as a badge of honor? Why not view it as the consequence of her continued love for her husband? If God did not take away her pain, maybe it was because he was honoring her character and her faithfulness, her love and her commitment to her marriage covenant. Why not, instead of seeing the pain as something to be eradicated, view it as the direct consequence of loving well?

"And why are you still mourning his going away?" someone might chide her. "Isn't it time you were over this?" Perhaps instead of absorbing the rebuke as if it were warranted, perhaps her response should be, "I continue to suffer because I cannot deny myself, because I cannot wipe away the years, because I continue to love and long for my wayward husband and friend." Perhaps she might go on to say, "If I must choose between denying all the life I have known under God with this man and the pain I now feel so keenly, I will choose the pain and live with it as long as it lasts!"

**There are a host of situations in life where pain exists only because the sufferer is fine and upright and compassionate and truthful.**

It isn't wicked to ask God to take away the pain, but we need to understand just what we're asking. There are a host of situations in life where pain exists only because the sufferer is fine and upright and compassionate and truthful. The employee passed over because she will not play evil games, the citizen cheated of justice because he will not lie, the lawyer who earns little because he maintains his integrity, the student who suffers loss because he will not cheat. All who live godly in Christ Jesus will suffer.

We aren't called to pretend we don't hurt. But something happens to suffering if we see it as a badge of honor rather than punishment or mere mystery. The apostle Peter shows us there is a way to view suffering and to embrace it gallantly.[1] We aren't all called to face the suffering that comes as religious persecution, but we are all called to embrace suffering that comes as a result of our loving commitment to something or someone.

Had Job known his suffering was directly related to his love for God, he would probably have embraced it with strong joy. But then we would have had an entirely different book, wouldn't we?

# Benjamin

✦

I heard a voice from heaven say, "Write: Blessed
are the dead who die in the Lord from now on."
"Yes," says the Spirit, "they will rest from their
labor, for their deeds will follow them."
—Revelation 14:13

A young boy came to me one day and told me he
had gotten in trouble with the principal at school.
I asked for the details—it was the kind of trouble a
twelve-year-old boy gets into. He was afraid of his father
hearing about it, afraid the principal would call him and
tell him about it, and what on earth would the boy do if
that happened? He said—with the intensity that only a
boy is capable of in situations like this—that he had
thought if he had a gun he could kill himself.

I put my arm around my son, George, and assured him that he could never get in such trouble that I'd want him to do anything like that. When he was gone, a great sadness filled me. What kind of a world is it—what kind of world have people like me made—when a little boy with wide and tear-filled eyes could speak with such intensity about killing himself over a boyish mistake?

Worry is the gnawing fear we experience in the face of possible loss. And there are so many things to worry about, aren't there? I'm not so dumb as not to know there are things serious enough to make us worry.

I chafe a little to hear isolated Bible verses about worry used to heap deep guilt feelings onto those who are worried over some very serious situation in their lives. Pounding the pulpit and berating people who worry isn't only bad use of the Bible, it gives the worrier something *more* to worry about! What we need is a better perspective, a new vision, another way of looking at things—even death itself.

Young Benjamin, so the story goes, was "awful feared of dying." It seems he was terminally ill, and in the way that children do, he picked up on what he wasn't supposed to pick up on. One day as he walked in the garden, looking anxious, a voice said, "What's wrong with you, Benjamin?" When he looked to see who had spoken, it was a flower. When he'd recovered from the shock of learning that flowers talk, he said he was terribly afraid of dying. At this the flower laughed and said, "You're silly. I love to die. I get to feeling droopy and weary, and then I die and wake up all fresh and new." Benjamin wished he could share the flower's view, but the only thing he could come up with was, "Well, that's all right for you, you're a flower—but I'm a boy."

On another day as he lay under a tree feeling poorly and worrying about what would happen, a tiny voice asked him what was bothering him. This time it was a caterpillar. By now the boy realized that all kinds of things talked if only people would hear them. "I'm awful feared of dying," he said, and the caterpillar rolled all over the place, laughing, like a tiny bell ringing. "You're afraid of dying?" he tittered as he hung upside down from a plant. "I love to die. I just wrap up in my covering, and when I wake up I'm all changed and beautiful. I can fly and everything. Dying is nothing to be afraid of!" The boy wanted to feel that way, to believe that story, but again, all he could do was murmur, "It's different with little boys," and he walked back into the house, still worried about dying.

One day he was feeling very tired, indeed, the sun was hurting his eyes, and he felt he just had to lie down; and he did. He fell into a deep sleep and when he awoke, he felt better, but he was still worried. When he walked out into the garden, he met an angel there. Though he had never seen an angel before, somehow he just knew this was an angel. "Benjamin, what's troubling you?" the angel gently asked. The boy said, "I'm awful feared of dying." The angel smiled and said, "Why, Benjamin, you be dead!"

Sad little boy did all that worrying and then one day he just up and did it and discovered it wasn't so bad!

Many people fear a prolonged and painful illness before death. They fear it not only because they have a healthy dislike for pain, they fear it for their family: the trauma, the helplessness, and, in some countries, the staggering cost of medical care. All that makes sense, but there isn't much that can be done about it. People must do what they can to get ready emotionally and spiritually before the day arrives. Suffering may not come, but death certainly will, and there's a definite approach we can make to that.

We can enjoy the comfort of our faith about death itself. "If we believe that Jesus Christ died and rose again," said a tremendous sufferer and martyr, "we know that our loved ones who have died in him are safe and well!"[1] And it's because people have found Jesus Christ, who experienced death for all of us, it's because people have found him persuasive that we find things like this written on gravestones: "Gone Away with a Friend" and "Freddie! Yes, Father!"

John Donne's magnificent poem, "Death Be Not Proud," calls us to a trustful defiance, and so does the way a group of Christians in ancient Smyrna marked their calendar. Polycarp, their old and much loved leader, had calmly refused to choose life if it meant spurning Jesus Christ—so he cheerfully chose death in the fire. The young church at Smyrna recorded the event this way: "Polycarp was martyred, Statius Quadratus being proconsul of Asia, and Jesus Christ being King for ever."[2]

Death is overrated. If even half of what we sing is true, if even half of what we pray is true, if any of the central truths we have learned about Jesus Christ are true, Death is overrated!

As Donne would put it:

> One short sleep past, we wake eternally,
> And Death shall be no more:
> Death, thou shalt die![3]

Trium

umph

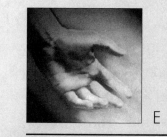

EIGHT

# TRIUMPH

It may be that [God] has
the eternal appetite of
infancy; for we have
sinned and grown old,
and our Father is
younger than we.

      —G. K. Chesterton

     ◆

# The Sea Gull and the Storm

✦

No, in all these things we are more than
conquerors through him who loved us.

—Romans 8:37

The Bible nowhere suggests we should not work to
alleviate the suffering of people. The reverse is true.
Again and again we hear condemnation for those who see
their neighbors in need but who stand by and do nothing.[1] The Christ assures us that judgment will involve
what we did or did not do for those in pain and need.[2]

It irritates us when people too quickly speak of the
blessings that arise out of suffering. It isn't only sensitive
agnostics like Albert Camus, in his book *The Plague,* who

think we should alleviate suffering before we extol its virtues. Even though talking about the blessings of suffering has its risks, the Christ is perfectly willing to do it: "Blessed are those that are persecuted for righteousness sake."[3] And Peter insists that troubles can result in a proven faith that is more precious than gold to those who have it.[4] It wouldn't be hard to parade a very long line of people, stretching back through the centuries, who would tell us with voices ringing that their lives were enriched immeasurably when suffering came their way. All things *do* work together for good to those who love the Lord and are called according to his purpose.[5]

I'd hardly suggest that God is in the business of afflicting babies with organ-eating parasites or pushing little old ladies under buses; but in a world where trouble and disease exist, he *is* in the business of turning these tragedies into occasions for good.

As you leave Belfast, going east toward Cultra, Helen's Bay, and Bangor, you quickly come to Holywood. That's where Ethel and I live, on the coast, and only about four hundred yards from the Belfast Lough which is part of the Irish sea. One of the real pleasures of life, for me, is to dress for the weather and walk along the seafront on a path I think runs all the way down the coast—as far as any sane man or woman would want to walk. I like it on our occasional bright days, but I really like it on wild, wet days. I'm a bit afraid of the sea, but I'm fascinated by it just the same, especially when it's wild (and providing I'm not on it).

Several years ago a hurricane that had been off the east coast of America was moving our way and we were to get the tail end of it. That's what the meteorological people told us, and that's precisely what we got (and we didn't want any more than that). I dressed up, made my way to the path down by the sea, and battled the elements. Every now and then I had to lean into the wind and really work to make some headway. The sea was boiling, the rain was bucketing down, and the wind was shrieking like a banshee. It was a cracker of a day.

I stopped every now and then to be hypnotized by the chaos of the water, and that's when I saw him. He was sitting on a channel marker out in the water, and I had to peer intently to keep a clear picture of him. A sea gull. He was sitting out there, perched on top of a post, supported by skinny, little legs. His head and neck were sunk down into his shoulders, and he was looking around him with that superior look all sea gulls seem to me to have, as though they scorn everything and everyone in sight. And he amazed me with his total indifference to the raging elements around him—even though they tugged at his feathers, shrieked in his ears, and threatened to pulverize him.

As I watched, an outrageous gust of wind hit him full force and lifted him right off the post. But at the very moment the wind hit him, he spread his wings, used the wind, and floated right back to where he was before. Down went the head and neck into the shoulders and back came the scornful look as he glared all around him.

**I saw a skinny-legged little handful of life spit in the eye of a gale.**

I felt like applauding him. I'd just seen a skinny-legged little handful of life spit in the eye of a gale. I'd just watched a vulnerable little bird get what he wanted by using the elements that threatened to injure him.

I've seen God enable people to do that too. When I first met Dirk Clay, he was a wide-eyed young man who wanted more than anything else to be a preacher. But Dirk had a problem—he had a pronounced stammer, and the more nervous he became, the more marked the stutter. He actively pursued speech therapy as well as his ministerial studies, but there was no sign of improvement.

Terribly upset, weeping and shaking, he came to my study one day and began to pour out his heart—his frustration, disappointment, and pain. Since God needed ministers to teach people about him and since Dirk wanted to share those wonderful things, why wasn't God curing his speech impediment? I didn't know then and I don't know now. I only know we talked and listened to each other, and we prayed. Finally, young Clay said that if God wouldn't correct things, why then, he would just live with things the way they were and serve the Lord as best he could.

I didn't see him for several weeks after that. The next time I remember seeing him, he was sitting in one of the front seats while a Mr. Hollis Maynard was teaching a class of people to speak in signs so they could learn from and teach the unhearing! That's what he did with his speech impediment! He used it to move him into a ministry where the hearing people, like myself, are dumb.

I'll never forget Dirk Clay. It's been years since I've seen him, but the last time I saw him, he was teaching the Bible, without stammering, with his hands, to people I can't teach and from whom I am unable to learn the many things they have to teach me. He opened up a new world to himself and to the deaf, and both were blessed. I remembered the remark of the atheist, Nietzsche, who said: "Neglect not the hero in thy soul." And he insisted, "What does not destroy me, makes me stronger."

But it was from Jesus Christ that Clay learned his life's lesson—from Jesus Christ who assured all the noble-hearted that in a world filled with raging storms, they can have peace in him. Such people have found that the very thought of him has enabled them to bear and use affliction in the service of others. That's how he used his own storm at Golgotha, to bring help and rescue to countless people battered by the storms of life.

I always enjoyed those walks around the coast, but that was one of the special days—the day I saw a sea gull whip a storm by using it!

# Doomed to Live

✦

For it has been granted to you on behalf of

Christ not only to believe on him,

but also to suffer for him.

—Philippians 1:29

Very well, he is in your power; only spare his life,"[1] said God to Satan.

"Why is light given to one in misery, and life to the bitter in soul, who long for death, but it does not come, and dig for it more than for hidden treasures; who rejoice exceedingly, and are glad when they find the grave? Why

279

is light given to one who cannot see the way, whom God has fenced in?"[2] This Job moaned in his abysmal misery.

Later when Job says that God has hedged him in, he will have something more sinister in mind. Here he simply wonders why God hasn't gone all the way with him and taken his life. Job thinks it would be a kindness from God if he were to end the miserable existence he was now enduring.

And is it really hard to understand why someone would be glad to see the grave who was being ground to powder, for whom every morning came too soon and every night was only the same torment with the lights now out?

Haven't most of us, in passing anyway, in our emotional weariness, felt some sympathy with the pathetic Swinburne when he said:

> From too much love of living,
>     from hope and fear set free,
> We thank with brief thanksgiving
>     whatever gods may be
> That no life lives for ever;
> That dead men rise up never;
> That even the weariest river
> Winds somewhere safe to the sea.[3]

The atheist was wrong, but it isn't hard to see Job going along with Swinburne's long poetic sigh. Still, dying wasn't for Job.

And why was he "doomed to live"? In this case, humanity is on trial. The Cynic had cast doubt not only on the genuineness of Job's devotion, he had said every human was self-serving and Job was the prime illustration. That's why Job didn't die! He doesn't die because he is the witness on earth of gallant and genuine character.

He is the proof that God can be loved because he is himself and not just a cosmic meal ticket. He is kept alive, said Princeton professor Paul Scherer, "lest there be no foothold left on earth for the soul's triumph."[4]

And do we dare say that this could be true of others? Of you? Of your loved ones? Dare we say that you from whom health is gone, never to return, that you are left alive to bear witness to a gallant and noble devotion to a God who will not make pets of us? Would it make you mad if somebody suggested that your loved one lingers over the weeks, months, and years, in depression as well as much discomfort, always in need of care—would it make you mad if someone suggested that she's left alive so that another point of light is kept burning brightly in a world so in need of it? Would you think it a terrible insult if someone thought that you're to live and not die so you can walk with God through your awful loneliness? Could it be that you're here to be another servant of God, "without pay," that the spirit of cynicism may be silenced and that God might be seen to be loved and trusted for himself and not his gifts or his protection?

There's no need to believe that God has expressly targeted people for this task (though that's not beyond belief since Job, Ezekiel's wife, and a long list of honored dead is before us in Scripture). Suffering comes often enough unbidden without us having to believe that God engineers tragedy. God isn't always directly responsible. But if tragedy comes, would it be insensitive if compassionate, patient, and wise people called us to embrace it and by God's grace to conquer it for humanity's sake?

I like what Henry McKeating, a past principal of Wesley College, said: "The book of Job teaches us that whenever humans live gallantly and cheerfully with suffering and do it in the name of God, they are somehow fighting God's fight for him against the dark forces of cynicism and evil in the universe."5

"Fighting God's fight for him." I love the sound of that! It adds luster to the pain and purpose to the suffering. Could it really be true? It was true for Job, true for Jeremiah, true for Jesus Christ. Resist the temptation to dismiss this. "Yes, yes, but all these people are beyond me, they're out of my league," you may say. "It's not for me to be one of God's warriors or to see myself as fighting his fight for him. All I can think about is myself, and besides, I've failed too often, disappointed him so sorely, and dragged my darkness into his places of light. It's too much to believe that I am one of those who help strengthen the arm of the Lord against the mighty."

If that's how you feel, your hurting heart, your confessional mood, your private tears, your repentant soul, your refusal to blame everything on others is proof enough that you haven't cursed God and died. To you, as to those other brave failures, he would say what he said on the night in which he was betrayed: "You are one of the ones that have stood by me in all my trials."6

Maybe that's why you're doomed to live and not die. Because God and humanity are on trial, and God needs someone to fight his fight for him.

# Though the Earth Give Way

✦

If the Lord had not been on our side . . .

the flood would have engulfed us,

the torrent would have swept over us.

—Psalm 124:2–4

I f we don't begin with the big picture, the little picture
will murder us every time.

Wasn't that what happened to the men on the
Emmaus road? They were able to see only part of the picture. They weren't taking in all that the prophets had said.

Isn't that what happens so often to us? Our fearful eyes
are riveted on what threatens us, and reality is shrunk to
this: ourselves and the threat!

"David thought to himself, 'One of these days I will be
destroyed by the hand of Saul.' "[1] So, during that time,

that's what it came down to—nothing but David against Saul. What of the promises of God? What of God's purposes? Where did God himself figure into this construction of the world? "One of these days I will be destroyed by the hand of . . . ?" My enemies are too powerful. I keep losing to them. All my fine plans are swept away when they approach—those inner enemies that undermine the foundations of my soul. My pride or lust or ambition or bitterness has me by the throat. It's sin or me, and I know it has me beat. My enemies are clearly too much for me, and if they are too much for me, one of these days I will be destroyed by their hand. My situation is hopeless.

So it's come to this—a straight fight between good and evil. God has decided to take no part? It's my lust and me—end of story? It's my apathy and me—God nowhere in sight? It's my fear-filled little heart against the thundering threats of life, myself alone? God nowhere around? It's the church against the world with God taking no side?

Wasn't it Albert Camus who said, "When it comes to a contest between the world and the church, bet on the world"? But it's never a straight battle between the church and anything! The church goes nowhere without her Lord. Christians face nothing alone. "I am with you always," is what our Master said.[2]

Our assurance of victory, our living hope, rests on remembering that God is always at the heart of things. It doesn't matter that our feelings don't go along with that! It would be nice if we always felt what we knew was true, but that's not how it is. It will have to be enough for us that God has given us his word that he will never abandon us or leave us alone.

To beaten, trembling Israel the word came:

But now, this is what the Lord says—he who created you, O Jacob, he who formed you, O Israel: "Fear not, for I have redeemed you; I have summoned you by name; you are mine. When you pass through the waters, I will be with you; and when you pass through the rivers, they will not sweep over you. When you walk through the fire, you will not be burned; the flames will not set you ablaze."[3]

God's people do not face the raging waters or swollen rivers alone. Israel may have looked at the Red Sea and thought, "We shall be destroyed by the waters" or at the swollen Jordan in Joshua's day, "We shall perish in the river." But God was there with them! The people of God may burn, but they will not be consumed.

These texts are more than words on a page, they are the sovereign Lord come to speak to us in our hours of peace, preparing us for the war. Coming to us in the hours of trial, assuring us of the glad outcome of it all.

We will not! We will not allow ourselves to be considered victims! "God is our refuge and strength," said the psalmist, "an ever-present help in trouble. Therefore we will not fear, though the earth give way and the mountains fall into the heart of the sea, though its waters roar and foam and the mountains quake with their surging."[4]

It's while their hearts are beating wildly, while the solid earth is giving way under their feet and they are

## Appearances mean nothing to the eyes of trust.

plunging downward to the boiling waves—it's at that point the psalmist says that God is "an ever-present help." Appearances mean nothing to the eyes of trust.

The storms of life may pound against the visible foundations of our lives, making them tremble beneath our feet. Health, friendships, finance, family, prospects, moral integrity, and sense of direction may all be threatened. But it is never the waves and me, it is never the earthquake and us, it is never me and Saul.

There is always God!

♦

# Clothed and in Their Right Minds

✦

The people went out to see what had happened.

When they came to Jesus, they found the man

from whom the demons had gone out, sitting at

Jesus' feet, dressed and in his right mind;

and they were afraid.

—Luke 8:35

I don't say we've all wallowed in sin since childhood, for by God's grace, some have been raised in the love and respect of God; and having been good children, they grew to be good men and women. It's true, just the same, that we have all come to the realization of our unlikeness to Christ, of our not-so-obvious selfishness; we have all shared in that original choice to turn from God and play god. And our light became darkness. Still, some of what follows will not make a lot of sense to those whose lives have been characteristically fine unto this very day. They will wonder if anyone experiences the trauma and war sketched here. But some have.

Some of us lived in darkness from the first, often unaware that our darkness was darkness until that day when conviction pierced us like a knife—that day when it exploded before our eyes like a bolt of lightning, illuminating the corners of our lightless world, exposing the corruption and the slithering, scaly things that bred and fed deep inside us. And even now, many of us who have come to Christ know more of darkness than we want to. We thought we were through with it, had baffled and beaten it by running to God in Christ.

The early days of deliverance were filled with such relief, newness, and joy that we were sure our dreams of holy freedom were altogether fulfilled. Then, with a sense of dread, we began again to feel familiar feelings, noticed our minds drifting to old haunts, and felt a growing irritation with a "freedom" that had actually bound us to serve even those we didn't care much for.

Maybe it's here that we feel our disappointment most. We thought if we were brought by God's grace out of darkness into his marvelous light that the battle against sin would be over. The promise we first eagerly accepted now seems to have been greater than the fulfillment. The men and women to whom 1 Peter was written had been born again into a living hope by the resurrected

> We thought if we were brought by God's grace out of darkness into his marvelous light that the battle against sin would be over.

Lord; why was it necessary, then, for him to call to them in terse words "Therefore, rid yourselves of all malice and all deceit, hypocrisy, envy, and slander of every kind"?[1] Why does he insist on telling them not to conform to the evil desires of their past life,[2] and why does he urge them to abstain from sins that continue to "war against" their souls?[3]

Are they free or not? Are they out of darkness or not? Are they in the light or not? If God is so powerful, if Christ is so victorious, and if we have run to him for aid, then why must we be shamed by a horde of biting and stinging defeats? Why must some of us be shamed and demoralized by our own evil?

Others wiser than I will have to answer these questions with satisfaction. I only know that he is able and willing to set us free—not only from our guilt, but from the power of evil under which we even now toil. And while it may not be today, our full victory is assured because he has left us prophecies and promises in the very lives of those he delivered.

Was there ever a wilderness so wild as the one inhabited by the man who called himself Legion? Was there ever a place so desolate, so stunted, so unpitied as the heart of the man who lived among the tombs? Was there ever such an arena dominated by the cruel and wasteful? Was there ever such a desert, barren of goodness and withered?

Then Jesus came. He turned the howling wilderness into a garden and made streams flow in the desert. A contemptible man now amazed all who saw him by simply sitting clothed and in his right mind.

But it wasn't this poor man alone whom Jesus cared for. "Go home to your family and tell them how much

*Clothed*

*and in*

*Their*

*Right*

*Minds*

♦

289

the Lord has done for you, and how he has had mercy on you,"⁴ he urged the grateful, transformed man.

And what good would that do the hearers? Would their rescue be as dramatic as his? Legion wasn't the only one who hurt himself and made his home with the dead. Were there not countless people who rocked in lonely misery and darkness? How does it help them to hear what Legion had to say?

Doesn't Jesus send him to his family and friends to assure them that what God has done for him, he is able and willing to do for them? To take their dead and self-destructive hearts, to take their pride and pomposity, to take their self-serving and sly approach to life and deliver them? Doesn't this delivered man become a promise of other deliverances? Doesn't he stand as a vivid prophecy of other transformations?

Of course he does! And how we need that assurance. There are hosts of us who weep when alone because the Christ hasn't come into the living of our lives and spoken the word of complete healing. He hasn't done for us the dramatic thing he did for Legion, and we sorely feel the need of it. But he did send the man and had him spread the word: the work of God has begun and will be completed in us all!

Is it any wonder, then, that Peter urges the suffering and struggling to "commit themselves to their faithful Creator and continue to do good"?⁵ Their hope is "living" because their Lord is living!

Holiness and wholeness will be theirs. One day, they will sit in the presence of God fully clothed and fully in their right minds.

# He Is Risen Indeed

✦

I am the Living One; I was dead, and behold I am

alive for ever and ever! And I hold the keys

of death and Hades.

—Revelation 1:18

I n his great mercy, the Father of our Lord Jesus Christ
"has given us new birth into a living hope through
the resurrection of Jesus Christ from the dead."[1] So the
apostle Peter shouted.

We can't pretend we haven't heard this message. We
can't pretend we haven't come to believe it. As deeply as
sinners like ourselves can, we hold this to be unshakable
truth. We haven't only heard the cry, "He's alive! He's
alive!" and wished it to be true—it *is* true!

We know he has triumphed over sin and pain and death; that isn't where the challenge lies. It is in our frantic moments, when we want to know why he won't ease our pain. We know he has good reasons for all that he does, but in our gouging pain and humiliation, we don't want to hear his good reasons for not acting, we want him to act!

We may sulk with Christ for not rescuing us, we may be angry at him for not doing what we want, but it doesn't enter our minds that he is lying out there in some unmarked tomb! Our complaining and anguish arise not from doubt that our faith is true, but from the fact that it isn't making any difference!

Holding it to be true that God has indeed committed himself to us and has shown it by the death and resurrection of his Son, we want to see him doing something more, like easing our pain and removing our humiliation.

I recognize, I think, that much of our religion is superficial; that we give glib answers to questions that demand more; that, as University of Nottingham theology professor Goldingay wryly comments, we can look at others and call their crucifixion a "challenge"![2]

But to pretend we are filled with doubt about our faith is not the cure for glibness. I don't care what Job did! If he slandered God, he was wrong! I don't care that he thought he was right; I don't care that his pain was almost overwhelming. As the book stands, God was being slandered. Why pretend we don't know what went on behind the scenes between Satan and God?

Don't tell me what it looks like; I know what it looks like. Just tell me that the Story about God in Christ is true, and the rest will have to make way for that truth. Why should we give more weight to our pain than to

Christ's pain? And God's pain? And God's loving commitment to us? Should the brutal honesty of the book of Job be allowed to obliterate the brutal but blessed honesty of the Cross of Christ?

Don't tell me that's easy to say when we're not hurting; of course that's true! But what's that got to do with it? If Christ really did die and rise again for us, what's the point in our pretending we don't know that? If we profess to have given ourselves in glad-hearted allegiance to God who has come to us in the person of Jesus Christ, how can we take seriously the claim that God might, after all, be the ultimate child abuser? Let's not pretend we don't know that he has given us his heart's blood in Jesus Christ!

The Corinthians were babbling on about the dead not being raised. Said Paul,

> If there is no resurrection of the dead, then not even Christ has been raised. And if Christ has not been raised, our preaching is useless and so is your faith. . . . And if Christ has not been raised, your faith is futile; you are still in your sins. Then those also who have fallen asleep in Christ are lost. If only in this life we have hope in Christ, we are to be pitied more than all men.[3]

But that was all said for argument's sake. He will bear it no longer and shouts with that decisive cry, "But Christ has indeed been raised from the dead."[4] He's alive! This offensive truth grinds to dust all the specious lies, all the plausible negatives, all the false conclusions. "All those terrible things would be true if Christ hadn't been raised," he says, "but Christ has been raised, so it's all nonsense!"

If the resurrected Christ is not the crucified Christ, we would be left unsure about suffering. If the crucified

Christ has not been raised, we would be of all people most miserable. But the crucified Christ has been raised, and we cannot pretend we don't know that!

Nikolai Ivanovich Bukharin, Communist propagandist and leader in the revolution, was sent from Moscow to Kiev in the early 1920s to address a vast anti-God rally orchestrated by the state. For an hour he harangued the people, using ridicule, abuse, and argument. Silence reigned when he stepped down. Questions were invited. A priest of the Russian Orthodox Church, one of the many sufferers, asked to speak and was given permission.

He stood beside Bukharin, faced the vast assembly, and gave the ancient liturgical Easter greeting, "Christ is risen." Immediately the whole assembly rose to its feet, and the reply came back like the thunderous pounding of a great wave against a cliff: "He is risen indeed."[5]

When the arguments are made, when the pain has spoken, when the heartache devastates to silence or madness, there still remains a fact, a truth, a Person: the resurrected Jesus Christ.

Now what?

# Notes

✦

## Introduction

1. *The Work of Christ* (London: Hodder & Stoughton, n.d.), 16–25.

2. The Greek text translates Mark 2:12, "in this way we never saw."

3. *The Works of Rudyard Kipling* (Hertfordshire, England: Wordsworth Poetry Library, 1994), 577.

## Chapter 1: COMPASSION
### Dead at Thirty-Two

1. Exod. 6:9 NRSV.

### Show Him Your Hands

1. *Imprimis,* (Hillsdale, Mich.: Hillsdale College) vol. 20, no. 11 (Nov. 1991).

2. Acts 10:38 NRSV.

3. Matt. 25.

### Shiny Boots

1. *Expositor's Bible* (Grand Rapids, Mich: Eerdmans, 1956), 3:679.

2. Isa. 32:2.

**The Hero and Mrs. MacIntosh**
    1. See Luke 22:28.

**Davie**
    1. "The Skye Boat Song," lyrics by Harold Boulton, *8 Selected Popular Scottish Songs,* vol. 1 (London: Boosey & Hawkes, 1932).

**A Card around His Neck**
    1. L. A. Banks, *Hero Tales from Sacred Story* (New York: Funk & Wagnalls, 1987), 65.
    2. Gen. 37–41.

**The Habit of Finding Fault**
    1. Paul Williams, "A Perfect Love" (Almo Music Corp., ASCAP, n.d.) from *Just an Old Fashioned Love Song* (A & M Records Inc. Beverly Hills, Calif.)
    2. F. C. Spurr, *A Preacher's Notebook* (London: Epworth Press, 1933), 63–64.

**Bill the Peacemaker**
    1. Harry E. Fosdick, *On Being Fit to Live With* (n.p.: S.C.M. Press, 1947), 154.

**"Pretend You Know Me"**
    1. *The Friend on the Road* (London: Hodder & Stoughton, n.d.), 113–116.

## Chapter 2: COURAGE
*"Merry Christmas, Father"*
    1. Matt. 5:11.
    2. 1 Pet. 4:16.
    3. Heb. 12:4.
    4. See Matt. 16:21–23.
    5. 1 Pet. 4:12.
    6. Jer. 12:1.
    7. Jer. 12:5.

8. Hab. 2:1.
9. 1 Pet. 2:24; Matt. 8:16–17.

### *I Will Do More Than Live*
1. Lloyd John Ogilvie, *The Bush Is Still Burning* (Waco, Tex.: Word Books, 1980), 101–102.

### *Captain Freedom*
1. "The Last Word," *Poetical Works by Matthew Arnold* (n.p.: Oxford Press, 1945), 410.

## Chapter 3: REDEMPTION
### *A Far, Far Better Thing*
1. Heb. 12:2.
2. See Isa. 53:10–11.
3. Acts 2:25–26 NRSV.

### *Grounds for Believing*
1. See 1 Pet. 1:22.
2. John 13:35.

### *Jessie Glencairn*
1. Frank Boreham, *The Three Half-Moons* (London: Epworth Press, 1929), 40–42.
2. Ibid.

### *Hastings Beauchamp Morley*
1. "The Assessor of Success," *The Best of O. Henry: One Hundred Stories Chosen by Sapper* (London: Hodder & Stoughton, 1952), 210, 212–213.
2. *Tabletalk,* vol. 14, no. 10 (Orlando, Fla.: Walk Thru the Bible Ministires, Inc., Oct. 1990). Under license to Ligonier Ministries, Orlando, Fla.

### *Maria and the Gangster*
1. Josh. 1:5.

# Chapter 4: Hope

### The Hope-Bringing Story

    1. Heb. 2:8–9a.

    2. 1 Pet. 1:8.

    3. 1 Pet. 1:10–12.

    4. Gen. 37:34–35.

    5. 1 Pet. 1:23–25.

### To See Jesus Is to Hope

    1. 1 Pet. 1:5

    2. 1 Pet. 1:9.

    3. 1 Pet. 1:3–4.

    4. 2 Pet. 3:13.

    5. 1 Pet. 1:7, 13; 5:4.

    6. 1 Pet. 1:8, 22–25.

    7. Cf. 1 Pet. 1:5, 9.

    8. Heb. 11:8–10.

    9. Matt. 18:8–9.

### The Prisoner of Chillon

    1. By Lord Byron in *English Poetry*, ed. Charles W. Eliot (Danbury, Conn.: Grolier Enterprises Corp.,1980), 2: 337–347.

### "I Am Lazarus"

    1. 1 Pet. 1:3.

    2. John 16:33.

    3. Rom. 4:25.

    4. "Poems for All Purposes," *Selected Poems of G. K. Chesterton,* ed. Stephen Medcalf (Pimlico, London: n.p., 1994), 209.

### "We Had Hoped"

    1. Luke 24:13–32.

    2. T. G. Long, *The Witness of Preaching* (Westminster/John Knox, Louisville, 1989), 125.

    3. 1 Pet. 1:3.

### The God of Good Hope

1. 1 Pet. 1:3.
2. James S. Stewart, *King Forever* (Nashville: Abingdon Press, 1975), 143.
3. 2 Thess. 2:16–17.

## Chapter 5: FORGIVENESS

### The Scarlet Letter

1. Ps. 32:3–5.

### Hear the Cry I Do Not Utter

1. James Hastings, ed., *The Speakers Bible,* (Grand Rapids, Mich.: Baker Book House, 1978), 18: 131.
2. *The Friend on the Road* (London: Hodder & Stoughton, n.d.), 105.
3. 1 Thess. 5:5 NRSV.

### No Record of Wrongs

1. Matt. 18:22.
2. Rom. 4:8.

### The Toys

1. A. L. Alexander, comp., *Poems That Touch the Heart* (New York: Doubleday, 1963), 92.
2. John Piper, *The Justification of God* (London: Independent Press, 1957), 25.
3. *God the Holy Father* (London: Independent Press, 1957), 27.
4. Matt. 7:11.
5. Mal. 1:6.
6. Ps. 103:9–14.
7. Micah 7:18–19.

### Bethelhem's Well

1. W. E. Beck, *Signposts* (London: St. Christopher Press, 1932), 24.

2. Francis Thompson, "Hound of Heaven," *The Poems of Francis Thompson,* Oup (London: n.p., 1945), 89.

## Chapter 6: CALLING

### The Incomparable One
1. C. S. Lewis, "The Horse and His Boy," *Chronicles of Narnia* (Middlesex, England: Penguin Books, 1971), 139.
2. Isa. 46:5.
3. Eph. 4:1.
4. 1 Pet. 1:14–15.
5. 1 Pet. 1:17.
6. Lev. 20:24, 26.
7. Heb. 3:1.
8. Heb. 12:10.
9. Heb. 12:14.
10. 1 Cor. 5:7 KJV.

### Is Nothing Sacred?
1. Col. 2:17; Heb. 10:1.
2. Ps. 139:7.
3. Ps. 2:11.

### "Be Holy"
1. Isa. 63:8.
2. 1 Pet. 1:16.
3. *Speakers Bible,* 18 (vol. 2):72.

### The Image of the Christ
1. *The New Redemption Hymnal* (England: n.p., 1986).
2. 1 Thess. 5:23–24.
3. *The Gates of New Life* (Edinburgh: T & T Clark, 1937), 245–246.

### Too Much Like "Saints"?
1. Luke 18:9 NRSV.

*Negotiations and Referendums*
1. 1 Pet. 3:17.
2. 1 Pet. 4:19.
3. Alexander Smellie, *Men of the Covenant* (London: Marshall, Morgan, & Scott, 1924), 339.
4. 1 Pet. 3:19–20.
5. Arthur Gossip, *Experience Worketh Hope* (Edinburgh: T & T Clark, 1944), 18.
6. 1 Pet. 4:12; see John 15:18–21.
7. Luke 9:22.
8. Luke 24:26.
9. See Matt. 4:1–11.
10. George Matheson, *Messages of Hope* (London: James Clark, 1908), 12–13.
11. 1 Pet. 3:17–18.
12. John 17:15; 20:21.

*Dead Heave*
1. See 1 John 4:16–18.
2. Leslie D. Weatherhead, *The Transforming Friendship* (London: Epworth Press, 1928), 33–34.
3. H. R. Mackintosh, *The Highway of God* (Edinburgh: T & T Clark, 1931), 171–82.
4. See 1 Thess. 5:23–24.

## Chapter 7: VISION
*What the Cynic Saw*
1. Clarence McCartney, *The Trials of Great Bible Characters* (New York: Abingdon Press, 1946), 90.
2. Job 38–40.
3. Job 1:8; 3:3.
4. See Matt. 9:9.
5. Num. 24:5.
6. *Law and Love* (London: SCM Press, 1940), 165.

*Formulas and Experience*
1. Howard Butt, *The Velvet Covered Brick* (New York: Harper & Row, 1973), 22.

*The Rewards of Integrity*
1. Norman V. Peale, *Sin, Sex and Self-Control (*Garden City, N.Y.: Doubleday, 1965), 91.
2. Harry Fosdick, *The Meaning of Service* (Nashville: Abingdon Press, 1983), 91.

*Gyp*
1. Frank W. Boreham, *The Silver Shadow & Other Day Dreams,* 2nd ed. (London: Epworth Press, 1919), 33–44.

*Things I Didn't Do*
1. Leo Buscaglia, *Living, Loving & Learning* (Thorofare, N.J.: Charles B. Slack, Inc., 1982), 75–76.

*A Badge of Honor*
1. 1 Pet. 2:20–21; 3:13–18; 4:12–16.

*Benjamin*
1. 1 Thess. 4:14.
2. James S. Stewart, *The Wind of the Spirit* (n.p.: Hodder & Stoughton, 1968), 55–56.
3. John Donne, "Death Be Not Proud," *Donne, Complete Poetical Works* (Oxford: Oxford Univ. Press, 1971), 297.

## Chapter 8: TRIUMPH
*The Sea Gull and the Storm*
1. 1 John 3:17; James 2:14–17.
2. Matt. 25:31–46.
3. Matt. 5:10–12.
4. 1 Pet. 1:7.
5. Rom. 8:28.

**Doomed to Live**
1. Job 2:6.
2. Job 3:20–23.
3. Algernon Charles Swinburne, "The Garden of Prosperine," *The Harvard Classics* (Danbury, Conn.: Grolier Enterprises Corp, 1980), 3:247.
4. *The Word of God Sent* (Grand Rapids, Mich: Baker Book House, 1977), 173.
5. Henry McKeating, *Studying the Old Testament* (London: Epworth Press, 1987).
6. See Luke 22:28.

♦

**Though the Earth Give Way**
1. 1 Sam. 27:1.
2. Matt. 28:20.
3. Isa. 43:1–2.
4. Ps. 46:1–3.

**Clothed and in Their Right Minds**
1. 1 Pet. 2:1.
2. 1 Pet. 1:14.
3. 1 Pet. 2:11.
4. Mark 5:19.
5. 1 Pet. 4:19.

**He Is Risen Indeed**
1. 1 Pet. 1:3.
2. Goldingay, *God's Prophet, God's Servant, A Study in Jeremiah and Isaiah 4-55* (Exeter, England: Paternoster Press, 1984), 29–30.
3. 1 Cor. 15:13–19.
4. 1 Cor. 15:20.
5. E. Banyard, ed. *Word Alive* (London: Belton Books, 1969), 27.